CHAKRA WISDOM ORACLE TOOLKIT

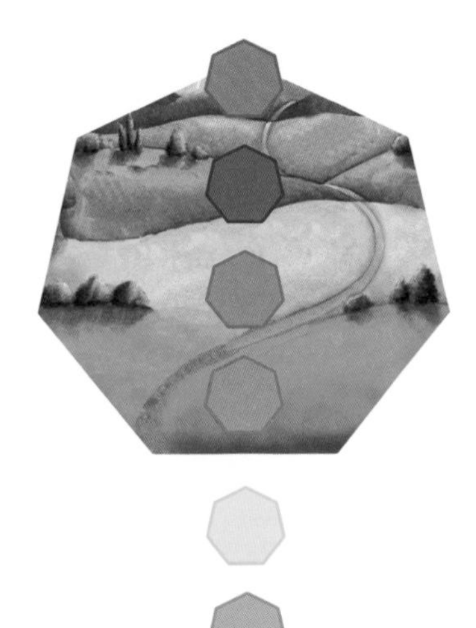

CHAKRA WISDOM ORACLE TOOLKIT

A 52-week journey of self-discovery with the lost fables

Tori Hartman

Illustrated by Gretchen Raisch-Baskin

Chakra Wisdom Oracle Toolkit
Tori Hartman

First published in the UK and USA in 2014 by
Watkins, an imprint of Watkins Media Limited
19 Cecil Court
London WC2N 4EZ

enquiries@watkinspublishing.co.uk

Publisher: Jo Lal
Senior Editor: Fiona Robertson
Managing Designer: Suzanne Tuhrim
Production: Uzma Taj
Artwork: Gretchen Raisch-Baskin

A CIP record for this book is available from the British Library

ISBN: 978-1-78028-829-1

10 9 8 7 6 5 4 3

Typeset in Gotham and Albertus
Colour reproduction by PDQ, UK
Printed in Malta

www.watkinspublishing.com

CONTENTS

INTRODUCTION

Allow me to say first how privileged and honoured I am to share this profound chakra journey with you. If you've decided to commit to this 52-week spiritual journey, you're probably already highly intuitive. Something in this book has called to you and now your intuitive energy is about to expand even further!

The journey you're about to undertake will give you the tools to change your life. Now, how can I make a statement like that? It's simple: commitment at this level will change you. And by embarking on a journey that will change your life, you'll establish a path of success to travel again and again.

My own journey began with a near-death experience in 1988. While I was recovering in the hospital, angels began to visit me, telling me stories. These fables were all different – as varied as the angels that delivered them – but I noticed that they were all based on colour. It wasn't until much later, when I started working with them properly, that I realized that these fables all represented our chakras (wheels of energy in the human body, each of which has its own colour). You see, after I wrote down the fables, I left them locked in a drawer for nearly 20 years until one day a friend in dire financial straits came to visit me. Coming on one of the fables by chance (it was the fable of the Carrot-coloured Clock, which became the Perseverance card), I showed it to my friend, who was inspired to create a miracle in his life.

I set up groups to work with the fables. From these, the themes and lessons of the stories emerged, and the exercises and meditations were developed. I'd always had an affinity for working psychically with cards, so it was a natural evolution for me to turn the fables into cards. It wasn't until I self-published the original divinatory deck, and began working with the cards, that I uncovered the full power of the fables. Someone once described the fables to me as "lessons without the lecture". Without preaching, they help us to understand the themes of life. They heighten our intuition and give us the spiritual tools to change our lives. They are miraculous because they make us see that nothing is impossible. They allow us to go back into the past to uncover the hidden agreements with our family of origin that prevent us from manifesting what we want and to work with what I term multi-generational healing, identifying the challenges and rewards passed to us by our family and more distant ancestors. These fables have helped me through my own dark night of the soul, more than once.

Chakra Wisdom Oracle Cards

There's a profound connection between this book and the *Chakra Wisdom Oracle Cards*, my divinatory system in which each of the 49 cards offers the insights of one of the fables. You don't need the cards to use this toolkit, but if you do decide to use them together you'll be amazed by the speed at which you progress and the high levels of personal mastery you can achieve. If you don't know how to read cards but have a wish to do so, I must tell you that by the close of this journey with the toolkit you'll know the card deck well. You can access the cards for free at www.ChakraWisdomOracle.com. You don't need a special psychic ability or to be a professional reader to benefit from this toolkit or the deck; your own intuitive expansion over the course of this year will help you to connect with the fables and the cards.

When Watkins published the *Chakra Wisdom Oracle Cards*, the idea was to give an abbreviated version of the fables that encapsulated the essence of their message, so that anyone wanting to work with the deck could simply draw a card, open the book and get a reading. Here in this toolkit, however, you'll find in full the original fables that inspired the deck. Each of the fables offers a spiritual tool for living and, week by week as you work through the fables, you'll add another of these tools to your kit. In this book we'll delve deeply into the magic of the fables that have transformed many lives, including my own.

Your journey

You'll notice that the fables appear in chakra order. In the first chakra (red), you look at your foundation and the source of your life energy. In the second chakra (orange), you explore your emotions. In the third chakra (yellow), you work on your intellect. The fourth chakra (green) is about opening your heart to your true desire. In the fifth chakra (blue), you learn about authentic self-expression. In the sixth chakra (purple), you work with your intuition. And finally, in the seventh chakra (neutral), you open yourself to finding your highest calling and reaching an elevated level of spiritual development.

In every class I teach, no matter what the topic, I always work with the chakras. I firmly believe in our intuitive wisdom with our own chakras. When you take this journey with the toolkit, you'll come to know your chakras in a very intimate and personal way.

I also believe all the fables to have three aspects: darkness, dawn and light (see pages 14–17). In the toolkit we'll be working with these overarching themes. When we're in the deep unknown of our personal darkness, we tend to be afraid and may think that a fable is negative. Yet this darkness signifies the beginning of a new awareness. It's the start of your journey into awakening your chakras, a gentle deepening of self. The fables come forward not to punish but to enlighten.

Dawn represents what's now coming for the first time into your conscious awareness. In dawn we open ourselves to the idea that something inspired is trying to find its way to us, even though life may appear to be challenging at the moment.

And finally, the light is the highest calling of the fable. This is where we choose the most inspired solution.

Are you ready?

Welcome to your journey!

Tori Hartman

HOW TO USE THIS BOOK

This toolkit is designed to take you on a magical chakra journey over the course of a year. There is so much more that you will learn than I can describe here. But know this: it will be *fun*. And challenging and exciting and, most of all, useful. You'll gain the tools to enable you to enjoy your life, navigate challenging periods and manifest whatever you choose!

The power of the fables to change lives is extraordinary. There are 49 fables, each a week-long journey. This leaves three weeks in the year to step outside the fables and look at overarching themes. On Week 1 we explore how to approach the fables through the concepts of darkness, dawn and light. On Week 23 we integrate the lessons of the three lower chakras and look forward to the higher chakras. Week 52 is the book's conclusion and an opportunity to review all the work you've done. Keep in mind that the 49 fables are divided into groups of seven, each group associated with one of the body's major chakras. On pages 10–13 I explain how each seven-week stage of your journey is coloured by the chakra with which the seven fables are linked.

Monday: read the fable

Each week is structured in the same way. First, you'll see a message of the week, along with my tip. These give you insight into how to approach the fable and the week's activities. Once you've read the fable, a first impressions section challenges you to ponder its meaning. You're also asked to set your intention for the week. I suggest you read all this material, then take a few minutes to think about your response to the story and write out your intention. This will set the tone for your week. However, it's important that you give yourself permission to do this *your* way. If all you can manage to do is read, that's fine. Just mark what you skip in case you feel the need to return to it later.

Tuesday: colour reflection

Today's activity is a contemplation that's often inspired by a question. As you read the colour reflection, keep in mind which chakra it addresses. As a psychic I get powerful impressions from colour and I think that's why the angels told me the fables in full colour. Open the door to the week's colour and allow it to speak directly to your intuition.

Wednesday: journal journey

I love the idea of a journal journey and the inspiration that comes when we allow our angels to speak through our pens. The journal exercise offers an opportunity to expand your instinct and allow inspired thoughts into your world. If you don't want to do a written task, sketch something or ask your angels for inspiration. Whatever you get down on paper in this process is divinely guided.

Thursday: make a connection

On Thursday, two exercises allow you either to open your heart to others or to connect with your angels on a solo journey. You can choose which exercise you prefer to do – or even do both, if you feel inspired to do so! Many of the exercises were developed in the early fable groups I led in my home in Los Angeles and are about opening our hearts to the possibility of our deepest desires occurring. How remarkable the results of these exercises can be was driven home the night I watched one of our members accept an Academy Award for their work.

Don't try to figure out the exercises intellectually. They were created in the magical spirit of play and can only be understood when you're fully involved with them.

Friday: meditation moment

Friday is the day when you allow your angels to carry you to an inspired place where you can absorb the lessons of the whole week. The meditation brings your awareness to the changes in your energetic state, aligns you with a powerful love of Spirit and frees you to manifest what you desire. Find a quiet place to meditate, where you will not be disturbed. Before you start, close your eyes and breathe deeply, letting yourself relax into a meditative state.

Week by week

There are no exercises on Saturday or Sunday because I believe that doing nothing allows Spirit to do its work. Everything that you've done in the previous five days will come together at the weekend. Sometimes the best form of meditation is sleep.

Trust that your process will be perfect. If you miss a day, keep moving. Don't delay your progress by thinking that you have to go back and do something if you miss it. That's old-fashioned punishment thinking. If you choose to go back that's fine, but don't pressure yourself. One woman sent me an email telling me that she'd missed an entire week because she'd spent it reconnecting with a daughter she'd given up for adoption years before. It wasn't until I pointed out that she'd skipped Penelope and Pickle - a story of grief, loss and true love - that she realized she'd got the entire week without ever picking up a pen.

Each week's fable has a different cadence. Always keep in the back of your mind what chakra you're on. Allow yourself to observe *your* story each week as it relates to the chakra and the fable. Decide for yourself how much time to spend on each exercise. Some days you may spend two minutes on it. On others you'll wrap yourself around an hour or more of writing or contemplation. Keep in mind that having fun is a huge part of the process.

The purpose of each daily activity is to add to your spiritual toolkit and find new ways of tapping into the power of your chakras. There are riches here beyond anything that you can imagine right now. However, your angels and your chakras know already how important this journey is - or you would not be reading these words now. The spiritual tools offered by the fables will heighten your intuition and change your life beyond anything that I can describe here. I encourage you to share this journey with a friend, or two or even more. Open yourself up to the idea of your own fable group - I can't tell you how incredible the lessons are when they're shared!

CHAKRA OVERVIEW

The chakra insights I offer are unlike any other chakra teachings, as I work with them intuitively. It's my personal relationship with the seven chakras that has allowed me to define each of them as a pathway to intuitive development. My biggest commitment is to support you in developing *your* intuitive power and finding your own internal path that will give you the tools to empower you and to change your own life. The fables have taught me that we all have everything we need to find our own path. In many ways my task has been to deliver the fables and then step out of the way!

I'm not someone telling you how to get enlightened. I'm someone who's been guided by these fables and who's here to share that with you. When we go on an internal chakra journey and begin to see how each stage builds upon the one before, it's astounding how much growth is possible. What kind of growth? The kind that shows you how to manifest what you want in your life. The fables help you do that. Only one caveat: you must allow the process and trust it.

Each chakra, represented by seven fables, will guide a stage of your personal evolution. As I teach the fables, over and over I have the profound experience of seeing how people come to embody the chakras in such a way that their lives become a complete joy. I'm not saying that they don't have challenges, but that they gain the ability to recognize their challenges, claim them without blame and forgive themselves for any self-judgment.

Some people see the value in studying the fables right away - and some people don't. Something pulled you to this work. Trust that. Trust yourself. You know if there's something deeper here for you. Trust it to reveal itself. Most people quit before the miracle. Allow yourself to travel on, even if you can't yet see where you're going.

Over the next few pages I'm going to outline the seven chakras and give you some ideas about how to view the seven fables associated with each chakra. I'll sprinkle in some of the concepts of multi-generational healing. Don't worry if these don't resonate fully at first. This toolkit is designed for you to return to as needed. If you stay on the train long enough, the scenery will change. Let's begin our chakra train ride!

1. Red chakra

Represents: your base. How strong is your foundation?

Multi-generational healing thought: Who taught you that? Do you need a better source?

Each of the fables of the first chakra represents an aspect of how you source your life energetically. Think about the roots of a tree and imagine your personal roots growing deeply into the earth. The energy that they soak up is the energy of your life. A healthy tree is rooted into good soil, with plenty of nutrients and water, would you agree? The red chakra fables show you the ways in which you create your own source and reveal how you're supporting yourself. They offer new perspectives and new ways of being. While you're in the red chakra allow yourself to create a new foundation in your life.

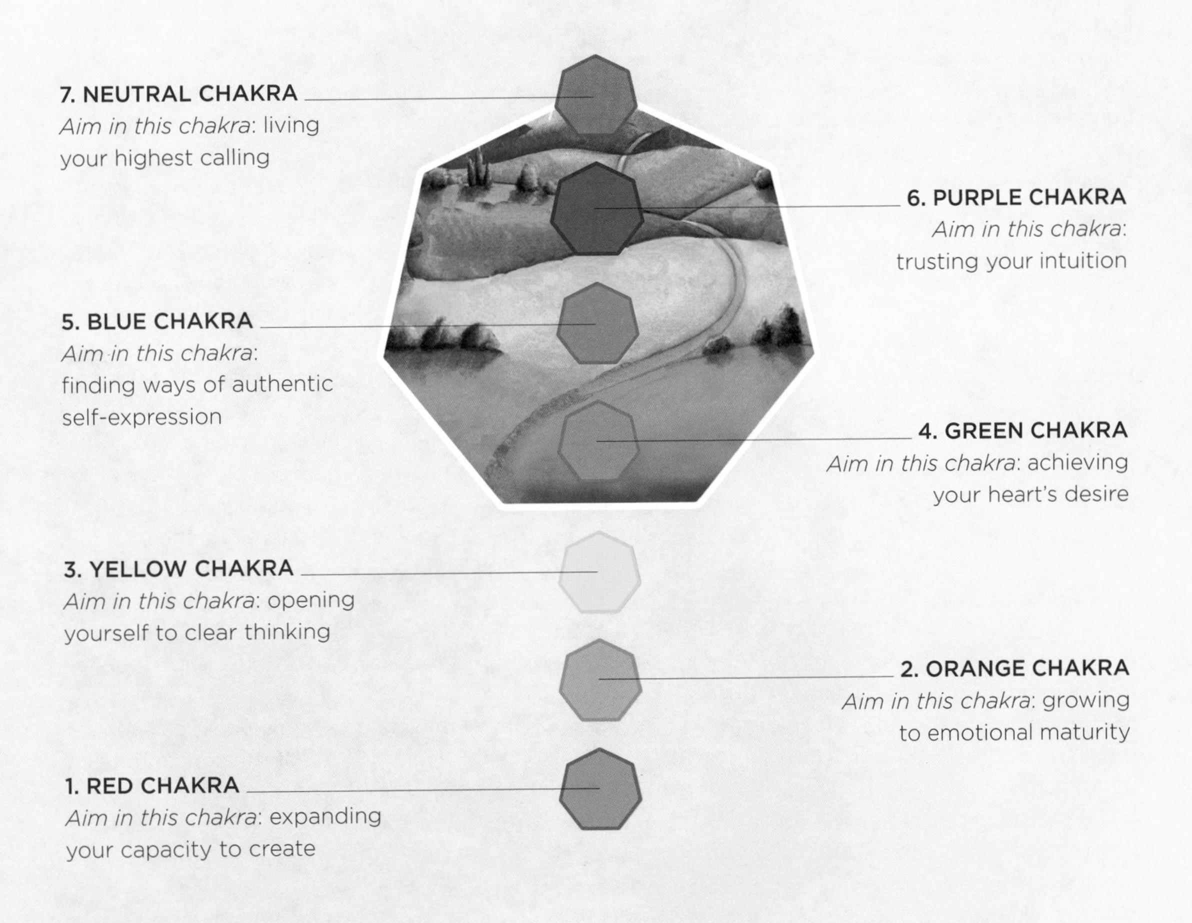

The overarching question to ask in this chakra is: "Am I creating a solid enough foundation on which to build my future?"

2. Orange chakra
Represents: your emotional life. Are you mature or obsessive?
Multi-generational healing thought: Did a grandparent withhold love from a parent? How did that pass down to you?

The second chakra relates to emotional matters. When we get stuck on our journey, it's often related to how we process our emotions in this chakra. These fables help us to understand that the way we deal with challenges is strongly linked to our emotional experiences. If you're often held up by your feelings, or even ruled by them, you may be sourcing your energy from roots that don't support your emotional life. Revisit the red chakra if necessary, as anything you were too busy to address there is likely to show up in the orange chakra. We need to understand how we're interpreting the experience of our life – that is emotional maturity.

3. Yellow chakra
Represents: how we interpret what happens in life. How clear is your thinking?
Multi-generational healing thought: Do you understand how you've made meaning of what you were told by, and witnessed with, your grandparents?

In the third chakra, each of the fables taps into aspects of our thinking, planning and following through and represents how our thoughts create our reality. Here, our rational mind either tricks us or supports us. Do your choices allow you to feel fulfilled? The fables of yellow may indicate how emotions have directed your thinking to this point. Look back to the orange chakra for insight here. Did you miss any of the work? In the third chakra you can see whether your actions support you and therefore where you're emotionally disciplined. One of the ways to empower yourself in this chakra is to recognize when your instinct is at play. Notice the thinking that lies behind your planning process and observe whether your day-to-day decisions are based on emotional maturity or immaturity. Enlightened thinking is the ability to observe how you act in your life.

4. Green chakra
Represents: how you relate to love. Are you open to love?
Multi-generational healing thought: Did at least one of your grandparents follow their heart? Or none? How did that pass down to you?

In the fourth chakra, we learn to follow our heart. These fables reflect different aspects of the heart, from heartbreak to heartfelt joy. In this chakra, we stop and consider if we're committed to what we're doing. To create or manifest anything, you must be grounded in your first three chakras. You need to lay down a solid foundation in the first chakra, find the tools necessary for emotional maturity in the second chakra and learn in the third chakra how to finely tune your instinct and elevate your thought process. Our capacity to love is directly related to the tools we gain in the earlier chakras. The green fables then offer ways to open your heart to what is true for you. If you ignore the warnings of your heart, what you attract in the upper chakras will not be sustainable or fulfilling.

5. Blue chakra
Represents: your self-expression and communication skills. What message do you send to others?
Multi-generational healing thought: What kind of life experience did your grandparents have? Can you see how your experience of life is directly shaped by your internal reality?

In the fifth chakra we begin to see how the world responds to us according to the energy we send out. The blue fables represent the way we express ourselves and how others see us – even who we'll attract or repel. Have you ever walked into a room and taken an instant dislike to someone? That was their fifth chakra at work! We're all constantly sending our message out to the world. What would your world look like if you were able to direct this consciously? These fables give you powerful tools to express yourself and help you keep the faith, stay on track and not give up on who you are. If your heart is opened from your green chakra work, then you'll be able to shift the way you communicate internally to make your dreams a reality. These fables, which each reflect different aspects of self-expression, reveal how your inner reality creates your outer reality and heightens your awareness of what's really going on in your life.

6. Purple chakra
Represents: your intuition and your sixth sense. Do you trust your intuition?
Multi-generational healing thought: Can you see how your grandparents may have created family issues that are still unresolved? How has this affected your life?

Each purple fable helps highlight unresolved family dynamics, as well as what you deeply desire. The fables here represent what has been hidden, so this is a time to focus on your sixth sense. They can even reveal hidden family agreements made before you were born. Many people find ideas about multi-generational healing challenging, so good for you if you can open yourself up to discovering more. The purple fables also deal with karmic issues and you may come to understand that you brought these into the world with you. In some ways the fables of the purple chakra represent the hurts that you're here to heal. I've also noticed that the sixth chakra concerns our ability to enjoy whatever we have created – or are going to create – in life. Pay special attention as you work with this chakra if you're holding another person (a parent, maybe?) responsible for your happiness or lack thereof.

7. Neutral chakra
Represents: living your highest calling. Are you willing to do the honourable thing?
Multi-generational healing thought: Did your grandparents make honourable choices? How does that affect you?

The fables of the seventh chakra represent the universal consciousness, which is neutral, and they are therefore neutral in colour. You'll notice that each fable in this chakra is without judgment. The neutral fables also represent how you relate to Spirit. The stories of the seventh chakra are lovingly offered as examples of the highest possible choices we can make as spiritual beings. In this chakra you gain the tools of spiritual freedom and an ability to connect with the universal consciousness. Not only will you be inspired and inspire others, you'll also be able to create anything that you can tap into energetically. The seventh chakra inspires what the first chakra must physically manifest.

OUT OF THE DARKNESS AND INTO THE LIGHT

Approaching the Fables

MESSAGE OF THE WEEK

What if you had the tools to go deeper than your thinking? What if you could listen to your subconscious and understand the messages it sends out to the world? Would that change your world? The answer is "Yes!" Over the coming weeks and months, you'll acquire many tools that will allow you, if you choose, to completely rebuild your life. Start here with an understanding of darkness, dawn and light.

TORI'S TIP

As we embark on this journey together, I'd like you to trust that you already know more than you're aware of. All you have to do is participate in simple daily practices for five days of every week, leaving two days free to integrate the material. Week 1 is the first of three weeks in our year-long journey in which we do not explore a fable (the others are Week 23 and Week 52). This Monday, I ask you to read the information about the darkness, dawn and light aspects of every fable and the concept of being in inquiry. The ideas that you absorb here will form the basis of each week's activities.

MONDAY

WEEK 1

UNDERSTANDING A FABLE'S THREE ASPECTS

Darkness

This represents your subconscious or the hidden aspect of the fable. It may also represent what's in the past and therefore what has brought you to this point. Often in the darkness you'll find a hidden agreement that's running your life – a repetitive pattern that's hard to shake.

Dawn

This aspect of the fable is what you're currently becoming aware of – what is "dawning" on you. It's about what is in your conscious awareness. The dawn also represents a sense of peace and love entering your world.

Light
This is the highest calling of the fable, its most inspirational aspect. Keep in mind that what may at first appear to be a "negative" fable may in fact contain the seeds of your highest spiritual awakening. In multi-generational healing, this is what I call the hidden gifts of your ancestry.

Each of the fables represents the idea of there being three sides to every story – yours, mine and the truth. This is also illustrated in the concept of darkness, dawn and light. Let's put these two approaches together. In the darkness is your aloneness. This is yours, what you bring forward into any circumstance. In the dawn we become aware of ourselves through the concept of collaboration. Here we become attuned to other ideas and outside influences, we can learn and undergo a change of perspective. The light is where the truth and our evolution live.

Over the next year, as you journey out of the darkness and into the light, you'll come to understand how you make meaning of events in your life. We create our reality from our vibrational body – the chakras – which guides us in our choices, consciously and unconsciously. How many times have you heard motivational speeches warn about negative thinking? "Be careful ... what you think is what shows up in your life!" And while that may be true on some level, the bigger picture is that the energy of your chakras creates your life experience.

In the darkness, we struggle for an answer – but an answer may not really be what we desire. However, in chakra work there's no conclusion, only a conversation. What if you didn't have to look outside yourself for your legacy or purpose? You don't. It's already in you. Multi-generational healing works by changing our perspective on who we are. What we all seek is a sense of peace, an awareness that our inner wisdom is working on our behalf. The point of this work is to be with yourself. Be in inquiry. Look more closely at this idea: if you're the querent (the questioner), the idea is to be in inquiry – *in quiry*. In other words, be with yourself. Throughout this book I'll refer to being "in inquiry". This means doing nothing but simply allowing yourself not to "know", to reside in the unknown. Through the darkness we'll wait together for the dawn. My father, a World War II paratrooper, had a favourite saying: "Don't over-run the drop zone!" That's what I'm saying to you. Don't rush to the answer. Waiting for the outcome in the darkness is often the most challenging work. This is where becoming a neutral observer is vital.

Set your intention for the week: Being a neutral observer does not mean being detached, which is energetically a form of resistance. It's about being an active observer of your own feelings. You don't attempt to get rid of your feelings, but you acknowledge them and take them with you. If you're waiting for payment for some work and it doesn't arrive when expected, then observe your own upset. You may say something to yourself like "Oh, I'm very upset." Then, feeling the upset, do something else, like wash the dishes, walk the dog or go for a jog. This week, set an intention to be a neutral observer. This is a skill you can bring to every fable. Think of being the neutral observer as the container that holds all the tools you will gather.

TUESDAY

COLOUR REFLECTION

What does the colour reflection say to you? Every Tuesday I will offer you a colour reflection, to give you deeper insight into the fable. Allow me to give an example from the red chakra: Demon Red Rainbow (Week 6). For many people, this fable about a demon is "negative". But what if it reveals the aspect of the red chakra that we need to strengthen? Looking at the darkness of this fable, we understand that we need to face our inner fears. In the dawn we find strength from a new source. And in the light we face our own inner challenges. Today, contemplate the idea that each tool presented here may have at one time been used as a means of survival and will require a change in perspective to be seen as inspirational.

WEDNESDAY

JOURNAL JOURNEY

Find your inspiration: If we're brought up in a challenging family environment, we learn early on how to survive. Unfortunately, many of these early exchanges are antithetical to who we are in adulthood. Many of us are still in that survival modality and continue to feel unsafe.

Imagine that you've been raised in a tribe that has given you the tools you need to survive. These tools allowed you to function in the world you came from, but now you're in society with people from other tribes who each have their different tools, many of which no longer work. To bridge this gap in understanding, we use a common terminology that's not really one-size-fits-all. We hear a lot about "abandonment issues", "not being available", "trouble trusting others" and "fearing success". My current favourite find is: "You need to get out of your own way." *Really?* I believe we have to *put* ourselves "in the way" to understand and shift what occurs in our lives.

Too often people attempt to get rid of an issue. My response? Whoa, wait a minute! This may be the very issue that you created to save your own life. You can't just remove it, like batteries from a radio, and expect your life to go on working. Often the failure of our attempts to change our lives is directly related to hidden agreements we had with our ancestors before we even came here.

Today, write out in your journal a list of sayings that you live by. Include the beliefs your family handed down, however outdated they seem. What have you been taught to think about life? Do you notice a pattern that indicates the survival mechanisms passed down in your family of origin?

THURSDAY

MAKE A CONNECTION

Connecting with yourself and others: Today in the solo and group exercises we're going to explore the value you place on yourself. How does the phrase "self-worth" resonate in your body?

There's an idea that self-worth is something we have to fight to achieve, but in fact it's not really something that we can chase after. We simply need to increase the parts of our life that we value - and a sense of personal value will follow naturally.

Solo exercise: We're all meaning-makers, but making meaning can leave us empty in the end. Why? Because the meaning we make of our experiences can be as useless as the survival skills we continue to use. What if these fables are a map to the tools necessary for a fulfilling life? Today, take some time to think about your map. What would you like to discover about yourself?

Group exercise: Imagine seven coloured keys on the table in front of you. One of those keys opens the treasure chest of wisdom that you currently need. Go round the circle with each group member picking one of the imaginary keys. State the colour of the key and pretend to open the treasure chest of wisdom, then share with the group the knowledge you need at this time. Allow others to give you feedback.

FRIDAY

MEDITATION MOMENT

Going within: This week we are exploring the idea of the three aspects of each fable. Over the next few days, allow yourself to observe how you respond when you meet with something that creates upset for you. Observe your own resistance - and allow it to be. This process represents the darkness of resistance, the dawn of the neutral observer and the profound awareness that comes with the change of perspective in the light.

MEDITATION

Close your eyes and allow the darkness to descend. This is the nothingness of the unknown, a safe place where Spirit can join you. Notice the peace within it. As you breathe, observe any feelings you have in this moment. Do nothing. Simply observe and be with yourself. Stay in the nothingness a while, for the wisdom of the angels resides here.

RENEWAL

Geranium

This Week's Focus: This is another beginning.

MESSAGE OF THE WEEK

We begin our journey in the red chakra with a fable about renewal. Beginnings, as Geranium shows us, are not always pleasant and can make us think that all is about to be lost. This week, consider where you are in the process of change. Read the fable and be open to new thoughts as you start on your magical journey!

TORI'S TIP

Refresh, releasing all pressure and fear. Allow ideas and a sense of rebirth to arise naturally. Be present and truly experience all the tastes, sounds and sights that come to you during this week. What will you take with you on your journey? Geranium reminds you that she flourishes in adverse circumstances.

MONDAY WEEK 2

THE FABLE OF GERANIUM

The leaves piled at the base of Geranium's pot had lost their colour and shrivelled into crisps. She watched helplessly as the wind stole her last beautiful petal from its stalk and hurled it into the neighbour's garden.

Just then, Geranium's owner picked up the pot. "Oh yes," Geranium thought, "I'm going to be an indoor plant!"

Moments later, she was pried out of her container and shoved into a smelly bag. "What's going on? Why am I being taken from the place where I was born?" Stretching her stem, she peered over the side of the bag to watch her owner putting fresh earth into her pot. New dirt! Wow! This was all right! She wiggled her roots in delight.

Her hope was dashed as her owner pushed new seeds into the earth. Geranium wilted a little more. "My pot!" she cried as she sank down in the bag. She wanted to scream, but Geraniums as a rule don't scream.

The smell in her new home wasn't so terrible and the exhausted flower surrendered to sleep ...

Geranium awoke. She didn't know how long she'd been sleeping for, but it seemed like a long time. She took a deep stretch and perked up when she saw the lush greenery surrounding her. She'd never had a view like this from her pot, that's for sure. It was beautiful!

She wiggled her roots. In the soil beneath the new grass she tasted coffee, and it was delicious. She tasted banana peel, too, and other good things to eat that people had thrown away. The banana was very ripe. Perfect!

The breeze was gentle on her petals. Petals? She was blooming! Yes indeed, in the middle of her life, a new beginning. And so, no longer restricted by her pot, Geranium grew and grew.

First impressions: What comes up for you as you read the fable? Is there a moral? A theme? Does the keyword associated with this fable, "renewal", express how *you* see this story? What do you see in the picture? Before we proceed, take a moment to write down your first impressions. This is your journey, so give yourself the space to process what in this parable speaks to you.

Set your intention for the week: It's easy to see three distinct phases in Geranium's journey of regeneration: her life in the container; her uprooting; and her transformed sense of a new life. This week, and during all the weeks of the red chakra, we'll look at your foundation and at how you begin things. The red chakra will reveal where you source from and how you motivate yourself. Set an intention for the darkness, dawn and light of Geranium by asking yourself these three questions:

1. If my outer reality is a reflection of my inner reality, do I need a new inner source?
2. What energetic source should I tap into in order to grow in a way that's best for me?
3. What feeling do I need to energize within to step into my new inspired journey?

TUESDAY

COLOUR REFLECTION

What does Geranium say to you? Before reading the paragraph below, write down three adjectives that describe this colour to you. Now read on ...

The orange-red of Geranium is motivating. Orange sparks are needed to create something. In Geranium there's a sense of urgency and a necessary action is indicated. The sweetness of a new beginning may be precipitated by an emotional upheaval in which you question whether you can handle change.

Did you write down three adjectives? These may help you to understand how you approach starting anew in any situation.

WEDNESDAY

JOURNAL JOURNEY

Find your inspiration: The prospect of change, of a familiar set of circumstances coming to an end, can be frightening even if those circumstances have made us unhappy. Yet the situations that generate our greatest fears often turn into wonderful opportunities. If Geranium has grown toward you, it's time to let go of the past and to trust that whatever is coming is better than what you've known to this point.

You may notice now how an old relationship or situation was limiting your growth. The indication is that you're ready to begin again. A new opportunity is coming from an unexpected source. Or perhaps something that seemed impossible to resurrect may start up again in a better way. Whatever is going on, regeneration of some kind is involved.

The excitement of new beginnings may come with a twinge of sadness. Whatever you're being pulled away from, know that you're heading for a better place. It's time to bloom again. If you're facing the fear of letting go, trust Geranium and know that there's a higher plan.

If things have been difficult for you in the past, remember that now you're different - because the circumstances are different. You're moving on! In your journal, write down how things *have* changed and make a list of the fears that you must face to reinvent yourself.

THURSDAY

MAKE A CONNECTION

Connecting with yourself and others: Opposite are two exercises about new journeys; one to do solo and one for a group. You may choose to experience your rebirth alone, but if sharing is more your style, try the group activity with one or more friends.

Solo exercise: Geranium marks a new beginning, often sparked by emotional necessity. What is it that you've wanted to create for some time now? Write down up to three items (more could be overwhelming, making you unable to do anything). Then ask yourself the following questions:

1. What do you know about how you start something – what does it take to get you to begin?
2. Do you like beginnings? Are they exciting for you? Why or why not?
3. If you do have trouble starting things, what did you do differently the times when you successfully created something?

Brainstorm on paper things that you absolutely know will help to support you in what you'd like to create. Now write down at least four reasons why *this* beginning is a different starting point for you. Does any one factor stand out as particularly important? If you have trouble with that question, think about what you did in the past to make something work. You don't need to find an answer immediately; instead, ask the universe for guidance and allow ideas to flow to you.

Group exercise: If you're working in a group, recall a time when you got "dumped". What did it take for you to see this experience as something filled with opportunity instead of despair? Ask the group for tools they've used to help them shift their perceptions. In addition, if you're currently facing a situation with any "charge" to it, brainstorm how to turn it into an empowering opportunity. As you do this, consider how your journey is different this time.

FRIDAY

MEDITATION MOMENT

Going within: Today's questions: Are you ready? Are you willing to be ready? Is there a long-lost passion in your life? Where is your renewal? Complete this statement: "If this week I experienced _______, then I would _______." Your journey and Geranium's may be similar – try this meditation.

MEDITATION

Imagine being discarded, like Geranium. Feel her fear and sadness as she surrenders to the inevitable. Now wake up in a new place. Notice how you feel. Let your feeling take you on a journey. Allow yourself to see and hear whatever experience is meant for you. Observe how you handle change.

SOULMATE

A Rose Without Thorns

This Week's Focus: It is time to face my true feelings.

MESSAGE OF THE WEEK

This week we notice our true feelings. Be the observer of your actions; like the man in the fable A Rose Without Thorns, you too are facing and expressing your new truth. Embrace the feeling and experience freedom.

TORI'S TIP

This is a week that calls for emotional bravery. Stand tall. What problems can you clean up? Who in your life needs to hear the truth in a loving way? A Rose Without Thorns indicates that a breakthrough is about to take place. Breakthroughs are often preceded by a period of painful resistance – can you breathe through this one?

MONDAY WEEK 3

THE FABLE OF A ROSE WITHOUT THORNS

Her beauty danced in his mind, a swirling flow of emotion. He couldn't take his eyes off her. He instinctively reached out and wiped her tear away. It burned his skin.

He'd played this part with her so many times he knew it by heart, but touching her threw his rhythm off. He knew her next line. She'd say, "How can you do this to me?" and he'd reply ...

"I love you," she said instead, breaking through his wall of thoughts. He stammered and avoided her gaze. He couldn't undo the effect of her words. It was too late. He'd heard her loving voice and now he longed to hear it again. She was so trusting, so open. Her sweetness filled the room, but before it could reach his heart, he cleared his throat and, like a trained actor, began to recite the next line of their script: "You're pressuring me ..."

Again, the words wouldn't come. He began to choke. What was wrong with him? He steadied himself and opened his mouth, but there was no sound. All he had to do was call her "too needy" – and he'd be off the hook.

She gazed upon him with a smile to lighten any heart, to cure the world's ills, to bring peace to all who encountered her.

This was the moment when he should leave, but he couldn't bring himself to turn away. He reached for her and buried his face in her hair, inhaling her scent. He wouldn't be without her. He tightened his grip.

"I love you too," he whispered. He wanted to stay. And stay he did. He'd found the freedom he sought.

First impressions: Now that you've read the fable, let's take a look at the illustration. Notice how the man's eyes are both closed, yet his third eye of intuition is open. In addition there's an eye in his hand of receiving and it's placed in the location of the seventh chakra – the chakra of higher consciousness. The implication here is that your soul knows how to build your life – and you can trust that. This fable is about solidly trusting the universal consciousness and your intuitive self to build relationships that empower you.

Set your intention for the week: Knowing the challenges you've been through, take time today to recognize the foundation you've already built for yourself. Is there a part of your foundation, your roots in life, that friends and even strangers notice and compliment you on? In order to invite love into your life, you must plant yourself somewhere it can grow. This week, set an intention to experience a deep soul connection and ask yourself what sort of life you need to be living to achieve this. Alternatively, complete this statement: "If only I knew how to _______, then I could _______." What roots do you need to grow to achieve your dream?

____

TUESDAY
COLOUR REFLECTION

What does Rose say to you? Even the most lovely flower conceals a challenge. A rose can be as hurtful as it's beautiful. The colour Rose brings deep passion with a tinge of sadness, its passion offering great emotional reward and softening any message. Rose challenges you to stand still and allow yourself to receive love. Today, with the help of Rose, name the truth that you must ground into reality this week. Remember, it's not the substance of the rose but the way its petals unfurl that provides its elegant beauty.

WEDNESDAY
JOURNAL JOURNEY

Find your inspiration: If a Rose Without Thorns has pricked you today, then you're most fortunate. As we mature, we learn that holding a rose close sometimes means being hurt by our inner thorns.

Whatever you've suffered in the past, remember that you're not facing the same situation here. This is the dawn of awakened feelings and the birth of a new truth. You're being presented with a different way of life. Trust that you'll know what to do. Stay open.

Time changes us all, if we're lucky. Surrender now and make the change. You want an incentive for change? Try love.

Make a list of the things that inspire you right now in your journal. Now make another list of what's at risk here, as you face your truth. Overcoming your discomfort will bring great reward. Hint: Breathe and stay grounded.

THURSDAY
MAKE A CONNECTION

Connecting with yourself and others: The solo exercise will establish what you really want right now and how to get there. The group exercise will uncover negative beliefs that may be shaping your relationships and replace them with positive ideas for being yourself with other people.

Solo exercise: Write down the one thing you desire most in life. By doing this, you're stating your truth to the universe and allowing your script to be rewritten. In the fable of A Rose Without Thorns, what happened next was not important, only that the man spoke his truth and changed his direction. The forces of the universe are set in motion by the truth.

Group exercise: Have each person in the group write down their true feelings and beliefs about relationships. Put all the papers in a bowl. One by one, pull each anonymous belief out and discuss it. See what new ideas can be created to support the development of new attitudes toward relationships. What would it take to powerfully own a new way of being?

FRIDAY

MEDITATION MOMENT

Going within: While at first glance the fable of A Rose Without Thorns may appear to be about an existing relationship, it's actually about someone who's never really experienced a meaningful partnership. The man in the fable has consistently played the same game over and over, avoiding real love in his life. This meditation is therefore about inviting love into your life or - if you're in an existing relationship - about creating the emotional depth that you seek. Remember that you'll only attract who *you* are. Your partner will be as beautiful and or as challenging as you think you are. You're close to making a major breakthrough - a real life change - if you'll only allow it.

The meditative thinking here is about emotional maturity or truth. It's about intimacy, which is *in-to-me-see* and something you get from yourself, not from anyone else. Complete this statement: "This week when I opened myself to intimacy, I noticed _______." In this practice I ask you to invite into your soul the truthful and brave part of you that's willing to risk everything for the beauty of true intimacy.

MEDITATION

In your mind, bring forth the light of Rose and stand in your vulnerability. Take a deep breath and keep relaxing until you find yourself in a safe place. Allow your mind to go blank. If you fall asleep, that's fine - it may be that your body needs to process this experience while sleeping. When you have reached a beautiful environment, the one where you feel most fulfilled, ask the Great Spirits to help you face that which you long for. Allow any nerves to pass. You may now know how to handle your present situation or this knowledge will come to you soon.

PERFECTION

Righteous Raspberry

This Week's Focus: I have the same high standards for myself as I have for others.

MESSAGE OF THE WEEK

There's a distance between you and your desires and you may even be putting up your own roadblocks. Take time this week to notice any self-sabotage. In this pivotal week we'll explore how to get to the next level of foundation-building in this first chakra. There's value in allowing yourself to be perfectly imperfect.

TORI'S TIP

This fable reveals what you're doing or what you're about to do. How does your perfectionist emerge? Watch out for your resistance – it may show up as being picky. The desire to change can cause extreme frustration when we try to hold on to a false front. Admit your pain, as this will bring freedom and intimacy.

MONDAY

WEEK 4

THE FABLE OF RIGHTEOUS RASPBERRY

Raspberry is naturally radiant and needs no make-up to accentuate her exquisite features, but she wears it anyway. She's a perfectionist. She's always adorned in a multitude of coatings, each one more elaborate than the last.

Raspberry sits alone, feared by many. She's only a small fruit and possesses no power to harm others physically. Many are attracted to her, but soon shy away once they get close. Why?

Raspberry feels the need to speak the "painful truth" at all times. Her honesty comes at you when you least expect it. Just last week she said to Mrs Orange, "I can't believe you dyed your hair that colour", and she told the Cantaloupes, "Your child is overweight." She believes from the very heart of her being that she's helping others by sharing her truth.

She's often been told that she's hard on others. "But," she argues, "If I don't tell someone just exactly how I feel then it's a lie. And I'm not a liar."

Her favourite, Elderberry, has pointed out on several occasions that she may not be a liar, but she's alone - because no one wants to be hurt by her "truth".

One day, Raspberry visited Elderberry. She chatted with him for quite some time before broaching the painful subject. "How can I get the other berries to talk to me?" she asked, hesitantly.

"Raspberry, I never thought you cared what they thought," replied Elderberry.

Raspberry sat straight up in her chair. "Of course I do."

"You prance around in your fancy fruit outfits pretending that you're the ripest berry in town," he told her. "And you never have a good word for anybody else!"

"I don't prance about! I just like to look good and those berries are jealous of me!"

"Go away!" He turned his stem on her. "You're not willing to listen to me."

Raspberry dug in her heels. "Yes, I am!"

"No you're not. You're too busy trying to be right. And, quite honestly, you're not very kind."

Raspberry fought back tears, "What does kindness have to do with people not liking me?"

"Everything." He sighed. "I give up. You still don't get it."

Unable to contain her pain any longer, Raspberry gave way to tears.

Elderberry said, "You're lonely." A nod was all Raspberry could manage. "I'm surprised that you, in your sweet beauty, have such a hard time finding goodness in others."

"I have to maintain high standards ..."

"For who?" asked Elderberry.

Raspberry's make-up was streaked with tears. She threw her arms around Elderberry and thanked him. He was stunned by her display of feelings. She walked home, oblivious to the stares of her neighbours. For the very first time, the true Raspberry wasn't hiding any longer. Mrs Boisen approached her. "Raspberry, are you all right?"

"Yes, Mrs Boisen, I am. Thank you for your concern." She smiled genuinely and walked on, without commenting on the tear in Mrs Boisen's dress. From that day on, Raspberry always looked for the unique qualities of other fruits and not for their bruises.

First impressions: What "story" are you presently telling? Often a story is an excuse. Defending a position implies that you're being attacked. If something isn't working out, notice it. Breathe. Allow yourself to step back. At least you've seen it. Escape your story by admitting your part in it.

Set your intention for the week: When you give up the need to win or to impress others, you can begin to be truly in serenity with yourself. This week, set an intention to stop defending, explaining or criticizing anyone (including yourself). What would your world look like without excuses? What if you simply owned reality? Complete this statement: "This week when I told the truth and allowed myself to be imperfect, I noticed _______."

TUESDAY

COLOUR REFLECTION

What does Raspberry say to you? As Raspberry combines the higher consciousness of violet with the grounding energy of red, its meaning is in learning to enjoy pleasures that are given to us by the Divine. Raspberry brings a determination to make manifest the universal consciousness and a spiritual confidence in decision-making. When you focus on what you're creating, and not on what's happening to you, Raspberry denotes a powerful inner shift and an ability to truly enjoy the moment. Today, reflect on a vision that you once only imagined and is now a reality. Recall your journey from bravado to humility to the vulnerability necessary for success. Complete this sentence: "As I step into creating, I can see how _______ was necessary for my journey."

WEDNESDAY

JOURNAL JOURNEY

Find your inspiration: Righteous Raspberry tells you to lighten up! Notice your present attitude toward others. Are you being too hard on yourself - and on others? Allow other people to be as they are. You'll never be satisfied if you expect others to live up to standards that are too high even for yourself. Allow others and yourself to do it wrong. Have flaws! Trying to make the world perfect will only exhaust you and alienate others. Allow things to simply be. Look for beauty and you'll attract it into your life. And remember that supporting those around you creates great allies.

In order to build a solid foundation, you must be willing to dig up some dirt. For years I've had a sign over my computer that says "Write it wrong". These three words have been the basis for every success I've had. Whenever I've written a book, I've just got something on paper and eventually I've been able to write my way into the project. We all must take a risk to get started. Take some time today to write in your journal the things that you could do wrong that would get you where you need to go. Complete this statement: "When I do _______ wrong, at least I'll have started _______."

THURSDAY

MAKE A CONNECTION

Connecting with yourself and others: Pick one of the exercises below to take stock of the ways in which you hold yourself back.

Solo exercise: Is perfectionism something that resonates with you? If so, write down the ways in which you are a perfectionist. Carefully review each item on your list.

How has being a perfectionist benefited you? Think about this and answer honestly. If you're a perfectionist then perfectionism has served you in some way. Does it provide what you need? If not, write down a few ideas about how to live differently. If you can't think of anything, then try writing as though you're advising your best friend on what to do. We often have all the answers for others!

Group exercise: List five things you do to avoid your goals. Share them with the group, discussing how these distancing techniques have served you. Ask for assistance in discovering what each item's underlying belief may be. What would you need to change to support yourself in moving toward your desires?

FRIDAY

MEDITATION MOMENT

Going within: Meditate for clarity. Find the good in your present situation. Worry is very contagious - and so is love. Which would you prefer to give/catch? Find beauty within and share it energetically today.

MEDITATION

Imagine that you are biting into a ripe raspberry. Allow yourself to relax and journey into the sensational taste of the delicate fruit in your mouth. As the bittersweet flavour coats your tongue, think about the people in your life. Find something good about every person who comes into your mind (no matter who they are or how you feel about them), before you release them. You will know this meditation has concluded when no more people come forward.

COMPLACENCY

Crimson Dreams

This Week's Focus: I am feeling the loss of my dreams.

MESSAGE OF THE WEEK

This week is about the importance of having a dream – and what it's like to lose your dream. To comprehend this fable fully you must experience it. This week we learn that what we deny is what will bury us. We see our shadows and step out from them.

TORI'S TIP

People spend a lifetime avoiding pain and sadness, when in reality these experiences help them to build a strong foundation for their lives. A kaleidoscope is jumbled pieces of colour, but beautiful to behold. Your life is this, too. If you journey deep this week, you'll clear much of what has been in your way, as well as determine if the dream you give up is even yours – or someone else's.

MONDAY

WEEK 5

THE FABLE OF CRIMSON DREAMS

The weather had grown colder and Flo's back hurt more than usual. She didn't know if she could bear another winter. She liked snow, but at her age she feared falling down. Her shopping bag felt heavier this week and the steps she'd climbed every day for the past 40 years seemed steeper today. Milt had been gone for almost a year now, but Flo still bought their weekly lottery ticket. Winning had been one of the dreams they'd shared. They won once. Well, Milt boasted that they did - just $100 but they were the talk of the building for a few weeks.

She and Milt had always planned on moving to Florida. But the kids lived nearby and Flo and Milt had wanted to stay close - just in case.

Flo's daughter, Alice, sat in the attorney's office; her husband squeezed her trembling hand during the reading of Flo's will. The attorney glanced at his very gold watch before he spoke.

"They could have afforded it, if they'd wanted to build. I don't know why they waited."

He was referring to the building plans Alice had found among some other papers. The plans for the home that Milt and Flo were going to build in Florida one day.

The money Flo had left would pay off the house that Alice and her husband had bought. At least they'd have it easier. For a moment, Alice imagined a vacation home in the mountains. Ah, maybe someday ... but not now.

The money was needed elsewhere. They'd have to put three kids through college, and they'd need a new roof on the house this summer. Her car was on its last legs. Yes, her parent's money was going to be put to good use.

Alice shifted uncomfortably. The bag on her shoulder felt heavier than it had the previous week.

First impressions: Do you notice how energy is handed down through the generations in this fable? The mother and daughter will never create a solid foundation on which to grow. It's important to see how this pattern can show up in one's life. The fable highlights how hidden agreements affect our lives; the idea that money must be spent only on "getting ahead" in life is a family pattern that's learned, not something we're born with. Are you affected by any unfulfilled promises from your family of origin? Are you ready to break the pattern now?

Set your intention for the week: Take a look at what you're currently pursuing in your life. Are you doing what you want to do? Or are you chasing an unfulfilled dream of a relative? It's time to reflect on what you truly wish to build in your life. Are your roots shallow? Or have you grown your roots so deeply that you'll be solid in even the biggest storm? Crimson Dreams invites us to focus on where we come from and what we'll build. This week set an intention to clarify your dream. What do you really want?

TUESDAY
COLOUR REFLECTION

What does Crimson say to you? Crimson is the colour of life-force energy and of deep contemplation. There's a tinge of sadness here, but Crimson has the ability to regenerate itself – like our blood, which is this very colour. Crimson calls forth the idea of family honour, but be aware of the trap created by an obligation to create something that's not your deepest desire. Today, think about what you're doing with your life. Ask yourself this: "Does what I'm currently doing call forth the best part of me?"

WEDNESDAY
JOURNAL JOURNEY

Find your inspiration: Crimson Dreams indicates holding back in some way. Are you selling yourself short? More than likely, if Crimson Dreams has stirred you, you may be at risk of giving up on yourself. Are you in that danger zone called complacency? Are your circumstances not what you really want? Crimson Dreams tells us that unless we're willing to take risks, we'll never realize our dreams.

This fable is about the need for a new awareness. Don't accept the demise of your dreams! This is a wake-up call to face your situation and begin to live the life you truly desire. Because you really can ...

Use your journal to explore the issues that keep things going in the direction they've been going. Drill down to the truth. The paragraphs above may offer clues for you. Step back and, as the observer, note down what needs to change. Sit with this. Wait. Only observe. Take no action today.

THURSDAY
MAKE A CONNECTION

Connecting with yourself and others: Can you be honest with yourself? Here are two exercises designed to uncover the beliefs that support complacency.

Solo exercise: In your journal, jot down a list of all the things that you're complacent about in your life. The fable of Crimson Dreams explored complacency in terms of being unaware of the dangers of comfort, of ignoring our instincts and of settling for something that's less than what we truly desire. Make your own list. It might include not wanting to change eating habits when food is an issue, for example, or overspending and always being short of money. Simply list the truth about what you're avoiding. This exercise isn't about feeling bad, quite the contrary. The aim is to lovingly see what you're choosing to hide from yourself.

Don't actively try to change anything. Simply allow yourself to feel and observe the sadness and receive the grace that comes from being with your truth. When you do nothing, you allow your angels to assist you. We can't heal what we refuse to reveal.

Group exercise: Imagine that you have a bag in front of you. Inside are beliefs that no longer serve you, which you've been carrying around for some time. Pull them out one by one and show your group what you've come to accept as your lot in life. Explain why you're still carrying each belief. Why did you acquire it? How does it serve you?

If it no longer serves you, feel free to discard it. Your bag will be lighter.

FRIDAY

MEDITATION MEANING

Going within: After you've experienced the meditation below, let me share a powerful idea with you. First, knowing isn't the same as believing. It's my view that all beliefs are fear-based. Knowing is a completely different energy. When you *know* something to be really true, you'll never need to defend it or argue for your limitations again. Take some time now to consider how committed you really are to creating the life you envision. Check inside yourself and ask: "Do I *know* that I can create this?" If your response is that you *believe* you can, you may be experiencing resistance tied to an unseen obligation. Part of our work in the red chakra is cutting certain roots when we're not growing in the direction we choose. Today, allow yourself to sever the ties to the root beliefs that have grown trees of doubt in your garden. Do this by imagining yourself cutting energetic ties and severing old roots. Notice that there's now room for new roots to take hold. These new roots are *your* visions and dreams - and no one else's.

MEDITATION

Imagine yourself doing the very thing you desire. Can you feel the joy of participating in your dream? Look back at what you are leaving behind to live your dream. Comfort the things or feelings you are leaving behind and experience your natural sadness at their loss. When you are ready, move toward the joy. Open your eyes. What has been revealed?

INSECURITY

Demon Red Rainbow

This Week's Focus: The greatest adversary is the one living inside me.

MESSAGE OF THE WEEK

From mild worry to terror, fearful emotions are rooted in your body, determining how you respond to any given situation – whether you instinctively choose flight or fight. Instead, centre yourself in your fear and use it as an anchor. This week you look at whether you're anchoring yourself before you act.

TORI'S TIP

The true story here is one of courage. When Demon Red Rainbow appears, it's a reminder to stand tall. This fable offers you a chance to recognize your old survival techniques. It's about that part of you that's trying to protect you – the part of you that needs love.

MONDAY WEEK 6

THE FABLE OF DEMON RED RAINBOW

Day after day, week after week, Bob McMullen worked on his inventions. He abandoned each of them after the chorus inside sang in unison, "It's useless, we say, now put it away."

"It's useless," he'd say aloud, before putting the latest project away. (Why wait to be rejected by friends and relatives when it's easier to do the rejecting yourself?)

Bob McMullen had trouble finishing things.

One day, quite by accident, Bob finished something. A vaccine that would eliminate fear.

Bob tested it on himself. It worked! He felt so good, so positive, that he decided to send it to a manufacturer. It would be a success. Yes, for sure. A success! It was then that the Demon Red Rainbow appeared before him. Demon Red Rainbow is the fiercest of all adversaries, because he lives inside our soul, soaks up our fear and makes it grow. Bob's vaccine had forced the Demon Red Rainbow out into the open.

The chorus inside him started up again, louder than ever: "What do you think you're doing? It's rubbish! Just throw it away!"

Bob McMullen begged the Demon Red Rainbow to go away. He put up a valiant fight, considering that the very sight of this demon renders most humans helpless. But the Demon Red Rainbow wouldn't relent. Bob grew weary, realizing that his fear would always be there, even if it were no longer inside him. Demon Red Rainbow wouldn't leave until Bob agreed to put his invention away. So Bob did. His vaccine hadn't worked. In fact, it had made the fear worse!

But the Great Servant had other plans. That night Bob dreamed of men and women whose lives had been changed by his miraculous discovery. In Bob's dream the Great Servant spoke to him of his vaccine's importance. "It doesn't work," said Bob, exasperated. "I still feel fear!"

"The vaccine allows you to carry on even though you are afraid," the Great One said.

"But it doesn't work! I wanted to get rid of fear!"

"I could never allow that. Fear helps you to detect real problems."

"But I'm afraid even when there's nothing wrong!" Bob shouted.

"Precisely. It is you who must distinguish between the real and the imagined."

On waking the next morning, Bob jumped out of bed and grabbed the vaccine. His invention did work! It had drawn out the Demon Red Rainbow and allowed him to face his fear. He carefully wrapped up his treasure and ran to the post office with the package.

Demon Red Rainbow ran beside him. "It's useless!"

"Maybe," Bob said, as he raced along the empty streets.

"The whole world will see what a fool you are!"

"Maybe," Bob said, as he slid the envelope into the slot. "But you don't get to speak anymore."

Demon Red Rainbow was shrinking fast. Bob was to have many more visits from his demon, but now he knew that the only "useless" idea was not listening to his own voice.

First impressions: No one likes the idea of a demon inside them, but what if you created it to protect yourself? In the red chakra you must face your inner demon to make breakthroughs in your life. There's nothing in the external world that's greater than your internal torture. We all have an inner demon, even people who don't appear to.

Set your intention for the week: The demon that lives inside us can turn out to be our greatest strength. This week, ask yourself: "How can I turn my inner demon into my best ally?" Set your intention to face what you fear most and be courageous in all your dealings. Ask yourself: "If I face what I currently fear, which is _______, what could I create then?"

TUESDAY
COLOUR REFLECTION

What does Pure Red say to you? The power of Pure Red to fire up a situation is legendary. Red instigates action and self-confidence. It connects with the part of us that calls forth the courage to see the direction in which we need to head. Today, look closely at what you truly want to create and decide what it will take for you to courageously move forward. Inspired by the sheer power of Pure Red, centre yourself before reacting to any challenges, to allow space for your personal courage. Ask yourself: "If only I could _______, then I would be able to _______."

WEDNESDAY
JOURNAL JOURNEY

Find your inspiration: If the Demon Red Rainbow speaks to you, it's an indication that you're starting to forge ahead on the path you've chosen - or that you will soon. You're correct in thinking that this path is important. Demon Red Rainbow denotes wonderful opportunities ahead, but you still need dogged determination.

If you're facing a hill that appears insurmountable, the Demon Red Rainbow reminds you that the strongest adversaries are those inside you. You must face your demons and things will improve. Don't abandon your focus no matter what comes up.

The best route to the other side of whatever you fear may be the direct one. There's a crucial lesson here. Know that the Great Servant always provides an ally when you face the Demon Red Rainbow. It will become clear to you who your ally is. You need not face anything alone. The Great Servant has chosen this difficulty for you so that you may teach others what you have learned.

Make a list in your journal of your current demons. When you've named them and faced them, you can gently coax them to become your allies. Use your journal to explore how this fable relates to your life and how your demons can help you.

THURSDAY

MAKE A CONNECTION

Connecting with yourself and others: Do the solo exercise to establish the importance of your dream/s. If you work with others, you'll uncover any hidden agenda/s that may still be lurking.

Solo exercise: Knowing the consequences of *not* doing something can inspire us to take action. What would you say are the five most important things you've ever experienced? List them down the left margin of a page, leaving room on the right. Keep it light-hearted. My list included chocolate and Bruce Springsteen! On the right side, say what we'd miss if we didn't have these things. Now, what would the world be missing if *you* didn't express your voice?

Group exercise: On a piece of paper, write down your biggest, brightest wish. This should be the one thing that, no matter what, you wish for with all your heart. With complete compassion, each person in the group now reads what you've written. Then tell the group why it can't happen for you. Are you aware of why you've prevented it from manifesting? Each person now tells you why your dream will happen, why it must happen, and how they'll support you in creating your dream.

Now imagine that your dream has come true. Describe how that feels. What would it take for you to feel like this all the time? It's the feeling combined with focus that creates the experience. State your intention to the group. Await inspiration from the Council of the Great Spirits.

FRIDAY

MEDITATION MOMENT

Going within: Demon Red Rainbow appears for a reason. By building a relationship with him, you can renegotiate his purpose in your life. You can also find a way out of the "I don't know why this is happening" self-victimizing conversation.

MEDITATION

From a place of peace, call upon two or three of your spiritual protectors. When they appear, express your fears. As fear enters the space, allow your protectors to form a wall between you and the Demon Red Rainbow. Allow your protectors to give you strength and assist you in becoming greater than your fears. Watch as Demon Red Rainbow shrinks to a manageable size. How do you feel now?

DISCOVERY

Pink from Pinkton

This Week's Focus: I am more than I think I am.

MESSAGE OF THE WEEK

This week, we'll explore the power of embracing whatever faces us in the moment. We'll also look at what it means to be conscious of our emotional experiences while they're happening. Like the trapeze artist, you must let go in order to move on.

TORI'S TIP

This week is about discovering that others are not trying to let us down, but simply revealing who they are. When you look closely at your own frustrated ambitions, you may realize that their purpose may be to inspire you to discover yourself and live your greatest life – a far greater one than you can see at the moment. Remember, what you plant now will determine your crop later.

MONDAY

WEEK 7

THE FABLE OF PINK FROM PINKTON

Pink was a strong, wilful young man. His mother would tell him that he was just like grandfather Pink (whom he was named after), founder of the town of Pinkton.

Things came easily for young Pink. One day he met Petunia, a beautiful flower who hailed from nearby Pinkerton, a suburb of Pinkton. From the moment Pink met her, he wanted to spend all his free time with her. His relentless pursuit of his heart's desire created a great love between them.

Over time, however, the relationship became too easy for Pink. He grew restless. He stopped calling when he said he would, claiming he was busy. The two began to spend less time together.

Petunia, in love, waited for him. Eventually she grew tired of waiting and left him.

Pink was stunned and remorseful. He knew that he'd been wrong. He tried for many months to woo her back, turning all shades of pink, but she'd have no part of it. For Petunia, it was over.

One day Pink learned that Petunia had moved away. He had no way of finding her and was heartsick for a long while.

And in time he healed. Years later Pink saw Petunia again. They ran into each other on the street, just after Petunia had moved back to the area. Pink was the happiest colour alive! His feelings for her hadn't changed. He invited her to dinner and they began dating again.

Petunia was more beautiful than ever. Pink was on his best behaviour - he wanted to show Petunia that he'd changed. He had, after all, done all his growing for her. But Pink sensed a difference in Petunia. She often didn't return his calls. Pink didn't understand. Why didn't she treat him well? Why didn't she care for him anymore? He was certainly kinder to her now than before! Pink was distraught. He went to seek the wisdom of the mighty Sky God.

It took two days and two nights to climb to the top of Pinkton Peak. Pink sat quietly for a long time before Sky God spoke to him.

"What's going on, Pink?"

"Petunia is revealing to me who she is and I don't want to see it," Pink sighed.

"Perhaps her purpose in your life is to inspire you to discover yourself." Sky God replied.

"I want her to love me the way she used to."

"Then you wish her to be other than she is," said Sky God. "You have grown. She has not. She cannot receive that much love. When you were absent, that was fine for her, for it was all she could handle. Now that you are present, it is she who must be absent."

Pink understood. "I get it. And to give any less love now would make me unhappy."

"Precisely," Sky God continued. "It's time to forgive yourself your past and for not understanding, and move on. There are great rewards awaiting you for the work you have done on yourself. Go from here and delay your life no more."

And so Pink left Pinkton Peak wiser. He released Petunia and, for the first time since he'd met her, he felt free.

First impressions: The fable of Pink is the essence of personal growth. How have you outgrown people, places and things in your past? Leaving people behind is part of our evolution. Could you be refusing to grow for fear of losing love – and at what cost?

Set your intention for the week: Are you trying to recapture something that perhaps no longer works? It may be time for you to venture into new territory. Take a moment to imagine yourself stepping outside your life and looking back into it. As you stand in a different consciousness and look at your life, can you see that perhaps you've outgrown what you're pursuing? Are you being truthful about what you really want from your present circumstances? Set your intention to get what you truly desire by planting your energy in the here and now.

TUESDAY

COLOUR REFLECTION

What does Passion Pink say to you? Passion Pink ignites the fire of desire. The energy of passion must be channelled or it can lead to obsession. When you notice friends being obsessive, it's because they're upset because something is not the way they'd like it to be and they're unable to free themselves from this ideal. The power of Passion Pink is the energy to accomplish arduous tasks and carry a commitment through to completion. Today, imagine that your desires are taking root. As your roots expand, imagine that what you truly desire begins to grow in front of you. You already have what it takes to create it, whatever it is you choose. Make a note of how you can focus your passion and use it to realize your dream.

WEDNESDAY

JOURNAL JOURNEY

Find your inspiration: Congratulations if Pink from Pinkton resonates with you. Pink shows us the process of developing self-awareness. It can be a challenge to admit that you've outgrown something, but being fully who you are is more glorious than trying to squeeze yourself into the past. If your current circumstances are upsetting you, it may be because you're trying to make something work when it simply can't. And the situation that you want to cling on to may be much worse than what you could have if you'd only let go.

Today, tap into your past and explore circumstances when it was painful for you to let go. Be willing to go inside and be with that part of you that was in pain. When you're ready, describe in your journal the outcome in your life after you let go of what was holding you back. Complete this statement in your writing: "Because I let go of _______, I was able to create ________."

THURSDAY

MAKE A CONNECTION

Connecting with yourself and others: Today's exercises are about new perspectives. In the solo exercise, you see how the pain of disappointment can be converted into a new energy. In the group exercise, you look at your life from the outside. What do you learn?

Solo exercise: Consider something in your life that has been personally disappointing. To master the emotional pain of this experience, stand with your feet firmly on the ground, reach as high as you can and allow your pain to mobilize you energetically. The energy you tap into by doing this will offer you a new strength if you allow it.

Group exercise: Write a letter about your progress in life, as if you were introducing yourself to a stranger. Who are you? How have you grown? Then send it to yourself. When it arrives, share it with your group. Enjoy sharing who you are. Afterwards, consider what you've discovered about yourself.

FRIDAY

MEDITATION MOMENT

Going within: Do this meditation to gain neutral insight into your situation. Stay open. Listen. Be willing to climb through whatever you face as you do the meditation. Regrets may surface – allow them to wash over you like a wave. Remember how strong you are.

MEDITATION

Imagine something that you are presently passionate about. Allow the feeling to well up inside you. Now begin a journey to the mountain of the Sky God. The way is steep and the going is hard, but you can make it to the top. The wind snaps around you and you are shivering with the cold, but your human worries drop away as you climb. When you reach the peak, spectacular shades of pink burst forth over the horizon. The Sky God joins you and begins to speak. Listen carefully.

ACCEPTANCE

Cherry Heart

This Week's Focus: When I accept myself, I find love.

MESSAGE OF THE WEEK

Cherry Heart helps you to look closely at the sources of your existence – the basis of your beliefs and values and how you are in this world. What points of view or beliefs do you hold? This fable also reminds you that you have a team of spirits rooting for you on the other side.

TORI'S TIP

Your ability to accept and love who you are is directly related to the meaning you make of your life. In other words, your sense of your own reality is shaped by the way you process your experiences. Notice in the fable how Cherry interprets the missing slice of pie.

MONDAY

WEEK 8

THE FABLE OF CHERRY HEART

The Great Goddess speaks: "Cherry was insecure. No other mortal could have caused her to be that miserable. She felt that something was missing from her life. This is a problem for many humans, who often put themselves down before anyone else can.

"Anyone who comes into contact with Cherry can see the warmth in her eyes. She works as a waitress, and loves it, but feels that perhaps she should be doing something more demanding. She cares greatly for the opinions of others.

"Cherry has a lovely apartment. Her car gets her where she wants to go and she has wonderful friends. She has a boyfriend, yet she senses (correctly) that he's unfaithful and this makes her sad. She longs for more with this young man, but he doesn't desire that.

"You must understand that, as Gods, we all follow the same code of ethics; humans must discover their own answers. We speak during meditation and respond to prayer, but we can't come too close. We can show signs, but if someone doesn't see them then we can't help directly. But I did go a little further with Cherry.

"One day in her meditation she again asked for her man to stay true to her. I whispered to her that if fidelity was what she desired, she'd have to go elsewhere - that was the best I could do. I thought she heard me. She certainly told enough people about her revelation, but she stayed with him anyway. Cherry has heart. She doesn't want to give up.

"And then, a miracle: one day a customer at Cherry's work ordered a slice of a freshly made cherry pie. Cherry cut the first slice then turned to another waitress and sighed. 'I feel that my life is like this pie. It's just great except there's a piece missing.'

"The other waitress looked at the cherry pie. 'Maybe,' the young woman said, 'You're just a heart-shaped pie, Cherry.' She laughed. 'A cherry pie.'

"Cherry stopped.

"Often humans think miracles have to be something spectacular - a lightening bolt. But those who understand know that a miracle is just the moment when a life changes.

"Cherry left her boyfriend and, after a while on her own, met a man who truly wanted to be with her. Today, she's very happy."

First impressions: Is there an area of your life in which you're stuck? Or a shift you wish to make? Cherry's perspective changed when she accepted herself. Perhaps your "missing piece" is the very thing that makes you unique.

Set your intention for the week: Complete this statement: "The one thing I'm missing from my life is _______ and when I get that I can _______." Set the intention this week that your missing piece will show up, so you can create a solid foundation for your life. This intention is important as this is the final week of the red chakra, before you begin the journey of emotional maturity in orange.

TUESDAY

COLOUR REFLECTION

What does Cherry say to you? The red energy in Cherry challenges you to move forward, to make things happen. Cherry is unsettling – not a colour for decorating your bedroom. Red is the colour of the life-force awakening in you. What's taking root in your life right now? Consider the growth cycle of the cherry tree for a clue as to where you are in your journey. Cherry needs the chill of winter, a time of lying dormant, before the regeneration of spring brings blossom. Leaves follow and then the fruit begins to grow until it's ready to harvest. Today, ask yourself if you're still in winter's hibernation or coming into spring's bloom. In the red chakra we consider the root, so ask yourself if you're trying to avoid the pain of a situation or if you truly understand that a deep winter chill may be the only way for you to grow. By being willing to go deep within, you will grow tall.

WEDNESDAY

JOURNAL JOURNEY

Find your inspiration: Cherry Heart reminds you that you may not be assessing yourself accurately. If you're drawn to Cherry Heart, consider that perhaps you're being given signs of a truth that you've yet to accept. Refusing to see the reality of your situation is self-defeating. By doing this you're short-changing yourself and holding yourself back.

This fable is about self-acceptance and seeing the miracles in everyday life. Cherry wishes to tell you that prosperity comes with self-acceptance. You're complete just as you are.

Today, consider just how complete your life already is. The fable of Cherry Heart is about distorted perceptions. If nothing needs to be added to or subtracted from your life for you to be complete, how can you give voice to what you feel is missing? If this fable resonates with you today, take some time to journal around the following statement: "I feel incomplete because _______ and when I have this I will _______."

What do you notice?

THURSDAY

MAKE A CONNECTION

Connecting with yourself and others: This week's exercises require a playful imagination. In the solo exercise you begin with the idea that you have a magical box of acceptance that will reveal something great about you. In the group activity you come together for a spiritual brainstorm to uncover new ideas and ways of being that will support you. Remember to have fun!

Solo exercise: The Great Goddess stopped by while you were reading this fable and dropped off a box of acceptance. Draw out one gift. Write down in detail what she gave you. Feel free to go to the box of acceptance and learn something really great about yourself as often as you wish.

Group exercise: Write down on separate pieces of paper the three things that you want most to create in your life (be sure they're things you really want). Then note underneath each item anything currently in this area of your life that's unacceptable to you. Throw all the papers into the group hat. Each person now takes a turn drawing a goal and its issue. One by one, each person stands and acts out the goal they've drawn, without using the actual words. (If you know whose issue it is, don't say so. This is important. In this exercise, each person's soul should be allowed to come forward safely without judgment.)

When the goal is guessed, the person acting it out also reveals the issue, then says "I can now accept this situation because ...". Another member of the group now has 60 seconds to come up with as many solutions as possible. Take a few minutes as a group to discuss other spiritual solutions. Continue until the hat is empty and all issues have found solutions.

FRIDAY

MEDITATION MOMENT

Going within: To know yourself, ask your spirit guides what gifts you possess. Once you've begun this query, follow up with an offer of your complete acceptance of another person, acknowledging the way they are in the world as amazing. Then try the guided meditation below. Afterwards, write out the statement "I accept myself" and place it somewhere where it will remind you to repeat the words to yourself every day for a week.

MEDITATION

Close your eyes and concentrate on the part of you that you don't feel is complete. With your mind's eye, imagine Cherry Heart. She's glad you came to see her and wishes to give you a slice of pie. See the slice you feel has been missing from your life. Allow it to become the gift you've always desired. Let your feelings create a new awareness for you. When you are ready, write down your new awareness.

SERVICE

Honey Adams

This Week's Focus: I attract to you whatever you desire, if you give up your desire.

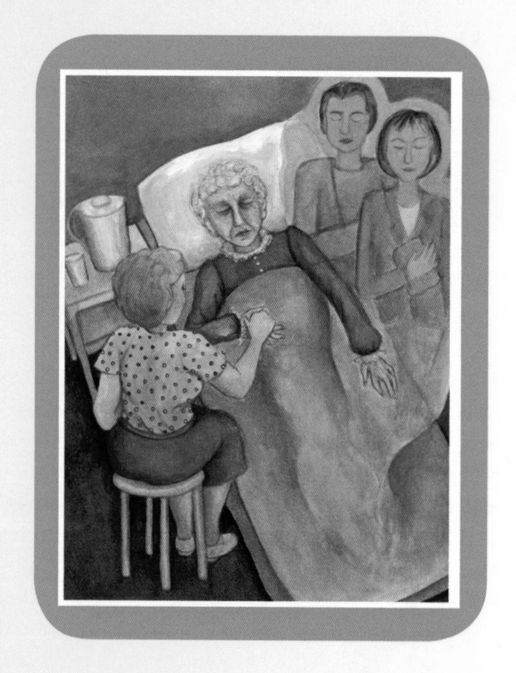

MESSAGE OF THE WEEK

For some, the word "service" conjures up the image of something forced and unpleasant. Honey Adams helps us to understand that service is an act of love and deeply felt by others. Keep in mind that we're now in the orange chakra, where the fables all deal with our emotional experience.

TORI'S TIP

The profound lesson of self-sacrifice can be challenging for those who have experienced a turbulent childhood. Yet service is the road to self-esteem. To build self-esteem, you must do estimable acts - service is the key. Allow this thought to become a part of your world this week.

MONDAY

WEEK 9

THE FABLE OF HONEY ADAMS

"I lived a long and rewarding life. I was a simple woman. Church on Sunday, holidays spent with family. Let all the kids grow up as they pleased. Charlie took my death the hardest. He was a good boy. I called for him and his boyfriend Timothy to visit shortly before I died, but they wouldn't come. I accepted them, but they wanted to sleep together in my house and, well, maybe I was too old-fashioned. I hope he'll forgive himself for not seeing me before my death. I forgave him.

"My Susie is a funny girl. She kept getting all these degrees and never used any of them. Said she hated men, then kept complaining she wasn't married.

"I guess my shy little Franny turned out to be the most like me. When she was little she never wanted to go outside and play. She'd sit quietly in the kitchen with me and my friends when they visited. She'd help me at the church functions; said she liked being with me. I loved all my three children, but I'll miss her the most.

"Franny was my pride. She truly became a good person. She never got a degree, but she made chicken soup for us when we were ill and cared for our animals just as well. From Franny, I learned about compassion, caring and love. She held my hand near the end and told me I could go whenever I wanted to. The very same words I spoke to my Joseph some ten years before. When my Franny said to me, "I'm proud to be like you," I recalled the times she'd volunteered alongside me helping those less fortunate, and I realized I was leaving someone very worthwhile behind.

"I'd wanted so much from my life, to be a professional and work in an office. I'd thought I'd given it all up for my children. It was at the end that I realized my dreams had more than come true. It was in giving up what I'd thought I needed that I found all that I desired."

First impressions: The fable of Honey Adams makes us aware of the subtle emotional connection we have with others. It also prompts us to think about our emotional relationship to the idea of service. Does anything upset you about this idea? If so, look back to where you're sourcing your emotions from in the red chakra. Is there any work that you've skipped over? If so, consider doing it now.

Set your intention for the week: What do you think living a life of service means? Being a volunteer? An artist who creates art to inspire others? Or something else? If you've grown up in a challenging family environment, you may experience service as a burden, because of what you've already had to do for your family. Set your intention this week to really uncover what service is – and could be – in your life. Consider that who you are and what you do on a daily basis can itself be a powerful form of service. Can you think of your career as a form of service? Love is also a service. Look at the deepest emotional connections in your life – these may give you a clue to how you value service. What you spend most of your time on indicates what you value most.

TUESDAY

COLOUR REFLECTION

What does Honey say to you? Honey's energy brings a sense of emotional warmth. The word "Honey" is used as a term of endearment and honey is the only food in the world that never spoils – there's honey thousands of years old that's still edible. Energetically that means staying power. There's a sincerity associated with this colour. It glistens in the sun and creates a beautiful reflection through light. Today, remember all those who've have made your life sweeter by reflecting their personal light. How do you use your emotional life to serve others?

WEDNESDAY

JOURNAL JOURNEY

Find your inspiration: Do you wish that your life could be different? So often we wish that things would change, rather than accepting them as they are. Honey tells you to take a good look at your present situation and make the most of it.

Giving doesn't mean compromising who you are. Being a giving person means bringing as much honesty and fairness as you can to any situation.

This fable reminds us to stop complaining, roll up our sleeves and get the job done. If you feel that you're being treated unjustly, you must act "just" yourself. Instead of wasting time worrying about what you deserve, concentrate instead on being of service. What any of us receive is up to the Great Spirits.

Today, consider that the relationships you've created thus far mirror your inner reality. To make a shift in those relationships, grow through Honey's wisdom by remembering that love is a service and so is doing the work you were meant to do. If you're a painter, writer, singer or musician, for example, know that it's a valuable service to be an artist. In your journal, write about how the work of others has enhanced your life - whether those others are people who love you or strangers. Stay with the theme that service means doing what you were meant to do, in whatever capacity.

THURSDAY

MAKE A CONNECTION

Connecting with yourself and others: What inspires you to give of yourself? Try the solo or the group exercise and allow the energy of Honey to expand love in your life.

Solo exercise: Take a moment to send your spiritual messengers out to the universe. Ask Spirit to bring to you the people and circumstances that will help you be of service in the highest order.

Remember that all your messengers are working even if you feel they're not there for you. When you've done this, find a picture in a magazine that represents inspired service to you. Put it somewhere where you can see it every day.

Group exercise: State one of your most cherished dreams aloud to the group. Whatever it is, can you look at this dream as a form of service? Whether your wish is to write a great book, start a charity or travel the world, see it as a service in order to create the emotional commitment needed to stay with your dream. If you're not sure how your dream could be of service, brainstorm some ideas with your group. Come up with five reasons why your dream would be of service to you, your friends or your family or to people you don't know. Once you've done this exercise, switch seats with someone in your group. This is an energetic way of switching your point of view.

FRIDAY

MEDITATION MOMENT

Going within: Today's meditation honours loving service. Now you understand that service is, at its core, profound love. Before you can give such service to others, you must love yourself. Honey Adams cares for herself deeply. She enjoys the simple things and is present in the moment. In my work I've discovered that it can be challenging for those of us who've had difficult childhoods to *not* feel that our lives are all about caring for others, so this new definition of service is about uplifting your soul. A definition of service must include the value we place on it. As you step into the next two days continue to ask yourself: "What will it take for my soul to sing? What will it take for me to be of loving service?"

MEDITATION

Keep relaxing until you find yourself in a place where you feel safe. Honey is there. She has come a long way to visit you. It doesn't matter what you say: simple words are fine. Explain to Honey why this place is safe. Now she has to go. She gives you a warm hug and thanks you for meeting her. Watch her walk into the light. What was the last thing you told her? Open your eyes and write it down. What does this tell you about your attitude to service and giving?

SELF-WORTH

Salmon Chair

This Week's Focus: "Come sit in my chair and feel my love," says the Great Servant.

MESSAGE OF THE WEEK

This week we work with our emotions around the idea of deserving. Every one of us is given the gift of self-worth, but when we try to hold others responsible for degrading this gift, we lose our emotional freedom. Thus the question of this week is: "Am I ready for emotional upliftment? Who do I need to let go of, to be free?"

TORI'S TIP

The Salmon Chair offers you a second chance at creating something you deeply desire. In order to accept it, you must stop thinking that your dream needs approval from others. This portion of your journey is about emotional maturity. As a rite of passage, you must accept the gift before telling others about it, thus making it real.

MONDAY

WEEK 10

THE FABLE OF SALMON CHAIR

Valley and River had surrendered to the storm. Snow was ripping through Valley, and River was being tumbled at a ferocious pace. A small child wandered deep into the forest. She wasn't lost, she was exploring, as children do. The wind stopped in the child's presence. In the icy silence of morning, a strong, salmon-coloured ray of light poured through the clouds and danced on the white snow to form the image of a large chair.

The child had begun to make an angel in the newly fallen powder, but she stopped, her heart thumping, at the sight of the chair. She'd never dreamed she'd someday see the great Salmon Chair. She stood silently, in awe of the beauty before her.

All children learn of the Salmon Chair; it's the great human quest. It's what you hope the Great Servant will someday reveal to you, in order that you may receive love. It's the most precious gift, though not everyone reaches out for it. River spoke to Valley: "Ah, the Salmon Chair has come."

"Hush," said Valley, "A child ..."

Only in winter could these two powerful forces talk. During summer it was forbidden because humans were all around and would listen. River and Valley had long ago promised to maintain the great silence, which enabled them to keep the divine secret of the Salmon Chair.

"There's no one there," said River, "You're always hearing things."

"Hush," Valley said again.

"I was about to say that while I protect the Great Chair, I never get to see it. Quite unfair, you know," said River.

Valley sighed. "There are those who can close their eyes and see it. Others have to climb mountains to view it. The Salmon Chair is not ours to experience."

The child, on overhearing this, was excited. She'd seen the mysterious Salmon Chair. She had to bring this knowledge back to her village! "I know the secret!" she squealed. River swelled and rose up, but couldn't reach her, high on the hillside.

The Great Servant calmed him. "This child is meant to know. The Salmon Chair has appeared to her. It is her time," he whispered.

Valley and River were both humbled by the Great One's presence.

The child turned on her heels and ran as fast as her little legs would carry her. She was determined, for she was meant to have the secret.

"Never question the path that great wisdom takes to reach you," her favourite elder would remind her.

But alas, it was not yet time for the elders to learn the wisdom of the Salmon Chair. For now the child lay exhausted from hours of trying to convince her elders of the ease of finding the Salmon Chair. They had, of course, not believed her.

In the darkness, the Salmon Chair appeared before her. She climbed in. She was meant to have it. And perhaps all was as it should be, for each of us finds the Salmon Chair in our own time, on our own path.

First impressions: Don't dissipate your energy trying to get others to understand your methods or vision. Sometimes we only want approval from the most disapproving person - don't bother! You're being given a great gift. Don't try to share it with those who don't get it.

Set your intention for the week: To have self-worth, we must experience the things we value. However, there are times when our need for the approval of others is so strong that without it our achievements are diminished. This week is about doing something completely enjoyable just for yourself, without feeling the need to tell anyone about it. Set an intention this week to do just that!

TUESDAY

COLOUR REFLECTION

What does Salmon say to you? Salmon is high energy and ready to take action. Salmon listens to feelings; in fact, it relies upon them. Salmon thinks deeply too. It doesn't react, it ponders. The lesson here is about going against the current, like the salmon that swim upstream. It may be important to contain feelings that are opposed to the facts. Remember this Chinese proverb: "Man who says it cannot be done should not interrupt man who is doing it." Your feelings may be going against your current focus. Salmon is all about using your feelings as an intuitive guide - and knowing when they may not be accurate. Today, consider how you can use your feelings as a means of tapping into your intuition. Can you step back from your feelings when they're not supporting you?

WEDNESDAY

JOURNAL JOURNEY

Find your inspiration: Salmon Chair may signify a love relationship waiting in the wings. It's your choice to receive it or not. Or a present relationship may be moving to the next level. This fable is about progress in the spiritual as well as the physical aspect of whatever you're now involved in.

Stand still and inhale love. Today, become aware of any attempts to avoid or minimize something amazing that's happening for you. To expand in the area of receiving, breathe in the magic of Spirit. Imagine yourself sitting in the Salmon Chair and experiencing the powerful light from above that fills you with love. Journal about the link between your personal value and the way you allow (or don't allow) your feelings to control you. Answer the following questions:

- When I'm upset, do I know how to soothe myself?
- Am I able to sit back in the Salmon Chair and observe my feelings from the outside?
- What if my feelings were guided to the highest possible state for myself and others?

THURSDAY

MAKE A CONNECTION

Connecting with yourself and others: By doing either of these exercises, become more aware today of the actions you take. Do they support your evolution in spiritual awareness or are they ego-based? Remember that aligning yourself with Spirit will attract more than ego can imagine.

Solo exercise: List a few things that are happening in your life and choose one you'd like to focus on. It can be an issue or a goal. Take no more than one minute to state your situation. Next, take a few minutes to write down several messages you think the Salmon Chair would bring you. Consider: What is the wisdom of the Salmon Chair? How does it apply to your situation? Then draw on the wisdom of the Salmon Chair as needed.

Group exercise: Each person writes down four intangible gifts from the Salmon Chair (relating to feelings and self-worth) on separate pieces of paper. One piece of paper is then drawn at a time, with the person who draws it identifying how this gift applies to them. The other members of the group then take turns telling the person who drew the paper why they deserve the gift. Does this throw up any changed perceptions that need to be adopted? Discuss.

FRIDAY

MEDITATION MOMENT

Going within: In this meditation, release everything you're holding on to that keeps you in a rut and doesn't feed your soul. Expand your connection to Spirit. You'll then understand the magic of the great Salmon Chair.

MEDITATION

Close your eyes and see the Salmon Chair. Breathe as you float slowly into it. Are you clenching your stomach? Let go of any tension as you fall like a feather into the Salmon Chair. Imagine the chair receiving you. Feel yourself being filled with Salmon light. There is no fear, only release. Stay there until you have received an abundance of energy from the light.

PASSION

Princess of Amber

This Week's Focus: I quietly sizzle and shine.

MESSAGE OF THE WEEK

This week we explore the possibility of transforming our lives through true passion. If you wish to inspire others, honour their opinions but don't allow anything to step in the way of your work of service.

TORI'S TIP

The Princess of Amber may visit you many times. It's hard to describe the magic of a true calling of service. You'll know it when you feel it. The Princess of Amber symbolizes being authentic and risking everything to live that way. What would you give to the world if there was no material reward for you?

MONDAY

WEEK 11

THE FABLE OF PRINCESS OF AMBER

There once was a young princess with a quiet passion for everything she did. She volunteered, visited the elderly and read to the blind. When she believed in a cause, she'd join protesters outside her own palace. Her spare time she spent caring for her beloved rose bushes; she even sang to them. She was not the kind of royalty who expected to be waited on by servants. In short, she was a *real* princess. Her behaviour caused disharmony with her father, the King.

One day, the *Amber Gazette* ran a story about the "oddball princess". It said she wasn't what a princess should be. The article chastised the King for not controlling his daughter.

Well, this concerned all the wealthy Amberites. They took up counsel with the King right away. The King must teach his daughter to behave like royalty, they said, or they'd push for an election and the monarchy would be voted out! (In Amber it was law that the citizens could elect their rulers if they wanted, but they never had, for they'd always been happy with the royal family.)

The King summoned his daughter and requested that she give up all her "hobbies" at once because they were hurting the royal image.

The princess contemplated her father's request for a long time – so long in fact that the rest of the family came looking for them. Finally, with the entire family present, the small princess spoke.

"I'm sorry, Father, but I must not – cannot – give up what I know to be right."

"You silly girl!" shouted her brother.

"There are plenty of commoners to volunteer!" cried her sister.

"My dear," began the Queen, "We can hire people to do your ... your ... 'work', then you'll have time to devote yourself to your roses."

The little princess sighed, "You cannot pay someone to feel passion or to know when something is right. I love my roses, but I love people more. My decision has been made."

The troubles in the castle became known far and wide. The Amberites finally forced an election, bringing the decision of who should rule them to the people. And alas, the King was defeated.

Much to the surprise of Amber's aristocracy, however, the people elected the princess who was so devoted to them. She was loyal to her family and asked that their lives would not change; she wanted them all together. She later married a prince from a neighbouring territory – and they lived quite passionately. Legend has it that her presence was almost hypnotizing, much like Amber itself.

First impressions: It could appear that Amber is a saint, but she isn't. She just stands up for what she knows is right, even if that means incurring the disapproval of others. Amber is aware of what she's risking, not just for herself but for her family. She's allowing her passion to be more important to her than her own family. This fable is about staying emotionally committed and not turning back. No matter what, in Amber we learn that Spirit lies on the road ahead.

Set your intention for the week: What are you willing to risk? If we live in fear of losing everything, then our passion isn't strong enough. Today, remember the things in your life that you knew you had to do, no matter what. Do you know the difference between an on-going emotional state of living in fear versus a temporary experience of fear? Set your intention to observe your emotions around this idea. Become aware of whether you're living in a state of fear, which immobilizes you, or simply experiencing fear, still capable of creating what matters to you regardless of your feelings.

TUESDAY
COLOUR REFLECTION

What does Amber say to you? Amber's brown is of the earth, rooted, deriving strength from within. Its orange allows you to combine that inner strength with powerful emotion. Amber's actions are well thought out; its decisions come from deep inside. It entices thought and calls forth the complexity within us. Its appearance shifts depending on how you look at it. Amber helps you to use your emotions to mobilize yourself into action, giving you fixity of purpose, determination and mental discipline. Today's question: "What emotion can Amber help me access so that I can step into a new emotional focus?"

WEDNESDAY
JOURNAL JOURNEY

Find your inspiration: The lesson of Amber is one of instinctual passion. The Princess of Amber is telling you to stand up for who you are and keep your eye on the work, not the rewards. Accept no compromises. When your intentions are good and true, you'll always land on two feet. You may be up against some pretty big odds right now, but you mustn't give in to what you know isn't right.

If you're truly immersed in your passion, then you're attracting people who support you emotionally in pursuing your dreams. The Princess of Amber is a reminder that it's necessary to act – to follow your passion – before you seek the emotional approval of others.

Take some time today to answer these two questions in your journal: "Am I willing to support my own passion emotionally, even if no one else sees its value yet? What will it take for me to focus on the task at hand and not divert my attention?"

THURSDAY
MAKE A CONNECTION

Connecting with yourself and others: The solo exercise involves creating your personal treasure map, while in the group exercise your passion is interrogated. Get ready to play!

Solo exercise: It's collage time! Using pictures cut from magazines and other found imagery, create a treasure map of the things that you feel excited about having in your life. Making this visual guide may take a few hours or even days - and you can keep on updating it as your passions shift. It's best to use a board that you can put up somewhere in your home where you'll see it every day. Then share your treasure map of passion with a friend. This is a hands-on experience, so avoid over-talking what you want in advance and just do it!

Group exercise: In this exercise, you get to speak as the part of you that's your passion. Another group member plays you and, as you, interviews your passion (played by you). Before you start, tell your partner what your passion is all about. In the interview, the person playing you must take care not to feed you any leading questions. When you're finished, make sure you both "de-roll", meaning state aloud that you're not the role you played. Here are a few questions that your partner might ask:

- What is it about _______ that drives you?
- Can you tell me more about it?
- Are you currently doing this?
- This sounds important to you. What will it take for you to really do it?
- Is there someone out there whose permission you need to do this?

FRIDAY

MEDITATION MOMENT

Going within: Take time today to discover your greatest calling - what matters most to you. When you answer the questions in the meditation, you'll become aware of the power that already exists within you.

MEDITATION

Ask yourself the following questions: What is my greatest strength? What are my challenges? How do I serve others? How can I serve myself? What represents love in my life? Close your eyes and invite the Princess of Amber to take a walk with you. What does she reveal to you?

GUILT

Saint Apricot

This Week's Focus: I am sorry but I have to take care of myself.

MESSAGE OF THE WEEK

The challenge of St Apricot is one of self-care. Our care for others can cross into doing for them what they should be doing for themselves. There are unspoken agreements within families and they often involve personal sacrifice. This week we look at the emotion of guilt and how to transform what's held us back emotionally.

TORI'S TIP

Honesty may upset others but it's an emotionally clean way to live. As we work with emotional maturity, we come to understand that someone else's reaction doesn't have to influence what we know to be right and true. Even the most sincere desire to avoid disappointing someone can lead to us being inauthentic.

MONDAY WEEK 12

THE FABLE OF SAINT APRICOT

Apricot was kind. *Really* kind. She was forever doing other people's work for them, and lending money that never got paid back. People were always complimenting Apricot on what a trooper she was. They said she was a saint – Apricot wondered if all saints felt as bad as she did. She felt trapped and lonely. She often stayed up all night watching television just for the company.

Her family told Apricot that people took advantage of her. Then they'd ask her for a favour. They'd berate her, saying, "You never do anything for your own family!", so Apricot would acquiesce and do whatever they wanted.

One day, a miracle happened. (At the time it didn't look like a miracle.) Apricot's latest collaborator, a friend, called and told her that she wanted out of the business. She felt that Apricot wasn't letting her express herself fully. She felt disrespected.

Secretly, Apricot didn't mind. Even when this woman showed up at all, it was Apricot who did all the work. But now her friend was talking about compensation for dissolving their "partnership".

"I don't understand ..." Apricot began, surprised. She knew that there was no partnership to dissolve.

The woman interrupted. "For one thing, I gave you the name of the project!"

Apricot put her foot down. "My mother gave me my name. Does that mean she gets half of what I make?"

The friend left, making no attempt to hide her displeasure. Apricot was hurt by her abusive tone. She wanted her friend back. But when she considered what had happened, a sense of relief washed over her. This person had never been more than a freeloader – she'd never really been a friend at all!

Apricot's sister phoned and Apricot told her what had happened. Her sister said that taking care of oneself was important. That made sense to Apricot. Then her sister changed the subject.

"Listen, my car is being fixed and I'm wondering if I could use yours for a few days ...?"

"No," Apricot said. "I wouldn't be able to get around myself."

Her sister was angry. "You do all this for others, but nothing for your own family."

Apricot listened patiently. "I can only give from my excess and not my reserve," she said. "I love you, but I need my car."

Hanging up the phone, Apricot realized that she didn't feel guilty. Her halo was gone.

First impressions: We often feel guilty over the disapproval of others. Guilt is programmed in us (often by our family) and can easily be triggered in other areas of life. Having read the fable, consider what triggers your guilt. What would it take for you to contain the painful emotional energy that comes when you face up to disappointing someone?

Set your intention for the week: Emotional maturity is our theme for the week. What will it take to be completely honest with those you love and let them know what your needs are? Freedom comes when we step out of that dynamic and take a stand for authentic connections no matter what the cost. Set your intention to be truthful this week.

TUESDAY
COLOUR REFLECTION

What does Apricot say to you? Ironically, as this fable is all about being impinged upon, Apricot is the most aloof of the orange family. This colour gives the impression of being friendly and available but also seems detached and quite content to be on its own. Apricot's power is that it offers a chance to look at emotions in a neutral manner. The ability to express who you really are is a gift given when you remain emotionally detached from the response of others. Today's questions: "Is there an area of my life in which I'm being less than truthful with myself? What can I do to step into the highest energy of Apricot?"

WEDNESDAY
JOURNAL JOURNEY

Find your inspiration: If Saint Apricot resonates with you, it may be because you've been, or are about to be, freed from a situation that has had you emotionally chained. This fable is a reminder to give from your excess and not your reserve. When we're emotionally drained we make promises we can't keep and disappoint ourselves at a very deep level.

We're also not giving from a true place of love if we're giving only to get the morsel of love that's offered to us. The people in our lives may not like it when we take care of ourselves, yet risking their displeasure is necessary in order to have a truthful relationship with them - and ourselves. Saint Apricot tells you that if you speak truth from your heart, then any guilt you feel is fear of being disliked. Remember, feelings of shame come up when we feel that we're bad; feelings of guilt come up when we feel that something we do is bad. If another person no longer chooses to be in your life, that's their choice, not your "fault". Honesty is freedom.

This fable is about a turn in your path. You're now moving in a new direction toward freedom. A gateway has opened to more rewarding relationships in your life.

When we allow ourselves to act out of guilt, we imprison ourselves and those with whom we're in relationships. In your journal, ask yourself: "What will it take for me to be emotionally mature? Knowing that those around me may not have that level of maturity, am I willing to be honest with myself and risk disappointing another person?" Hint: when you understand that an obligation has been a choice all along, you can draw on the strength of knowing that you chose it. And once you understand that you chose it, you're free to make a different choice.

THURSDAY

MAKE A CONNECTION

Connecting with yourself and others: Today, begin a practice of being truthful about time. If it will take you an hour to get somewhere, resist the urge to say, "I'll be there in 15 minutes." Instead, offer the truth and risk facing disapproval. This approach frees you from the guilt and pressure of being late. Now, try either the solo or the group exercise to reinforce acting from your authentic feelings.

Solo exercise: Make a list of your daily activities over the last week. Accompany this with a short written statement of what you really need and desire. Do your actions coincide with your statement? Decide which actions support your statement and which ones don't. Are there changes you wish to make? Use Friday's meditation to support your changes.

Group exercise: Ask other members of your group what they need in their lives right now. Can you help them personally or connect them with someone who can help them? If you're able to assist, do so. If not, simply say, "I'd love to help, but I can't." It's very important not to go into a story here about why you can't help. Notice how it feels to say "No". And how does it feel to be told "No"? Discuss these findings as a group.

FRIDAY

MEDITATION MEANING

Going within: Today, imagine what it would be like to live without chains and have no obligations in any area of your life. Is there a way to turn obligation into choice? Hint: just choose it!

MEDITATION

Imagine the chains that hold you down. As you relax, the links weaken one by one. See and hear each one fall to the ground. With each thud, see a chunk of fear or guilt fall away. When you are free, get up and walk into a glowing Apricot light. What happens then?

IMPASSE

Reggie Rust

This Week's Focus: This path is obstructed; re-route.

MESSAGE OF THE WEEK

Reggie Rust reminds us that an impasse isn't a "No", but a "Not this way". This week we're made aware of how we deal with emotional disappointment. Do we allow it to stop us? Or do we determine a new course of action?

TORI'S TIP

A seeming end to the journey and the old adage, "Where there's a will there's a way," comes up. A temporary stop or setback gives us the opportunity to re-evaluate our direction and discover flaws in our prior plan. Reggie is a reminder that the path you're on may not be yours. You'll be directed to where you're meant to go, so be the observer and don't force an outcome.

MONDAY

WEEK 13

THE FABLE OF REGGIE RUST

Clem and Craig were plodding through the mountains when Clem spotted the towering figure of Reggie Rust on the path ahead. "Damn it to hell, Craig, Reggie's there!"

"Naw! What we gonna do?"

"Nothin', 'cept wait." Clem sat down on a log.

Craig stood over his travelling partner. "Can't be waitin' here forever."

"What do you suggest? We could kill ourselves tryin' to get through! Cause I tell you what, Reg ain't gonna let us by." Clem pulled out his thermos and poured himself a coffee.

"Now I don't know what to do." Craig set himself down beside Clem. They stared at Reggie Rust blocking their path.

"Oh, heck," Clem said emptying his cup. "We gotta try."

Craig followed, but ten feet away from Reggie Rust they stopped again. Reggie said nothing, but his demeanour was clear. This path was no longer passable. The boys swore under their breath and returned to the log.

Clem patted his buddy on the shoulder. "Ol' Reg is just doin' what he's supposed to. He's stopped me a whole bunch a times."

"He just don't seem that smart," Craig muttered.

Clem shook his head and pointed at Reggie. "He's about as dumb as they come. All he knows is how to block a path. Hell, I suppose the Great Servant has a purpose for us all. And Ol' Reggie Rust's is to let us know when we can't go the way we planned."

"Well, now, that's pretty philio-sophical of you, but what we gonna do?"

"Wait here."

"For what?"

Clem laughed. "A new plan."

Two moons passed as the boys sat thinking. Finally, Craig broke the silence. "You know, my Uncle Sylvester owes his riches to Reg. He appeared right when my uncle was headin' off to start at a factory. But Reggie barricaded his path and he had to change his plans."

"Didn't the factory close?" Clem asked.

"Yup."

Clem leaned in, very interested in the story. "Hell, is that how he struck oil?"

"Yup."

"No foolin'!" Clem looked at Reggie Rust. "Maybe we need to go another way."

And the decision was made. When the boys were out of sight, Reggie Rust moved on as well. For the blocked path was a gift to Clem and Craig. Reggie was there to protect them from the landslide that would have cost them their lives.

First impressions: Reggie reminds us that not every path is for the highest good. We need to learn how to sit with uncomfortable feelings until a solution appears. This is another aspect of emotional maturity, in which you find your neutral observer, the part of you that holds still even when the world feels like it's falling apart. This is a vital skill learned in the second chakra.

Set your intention for the week: How do you cope with frustration? Are you a quitter? Your emotional response to setbacks dictates how you'll behave in any given circumstance. This week, set an intention to observe your emotions when something doesn't flow your way.

TUESDAY
COLOUR REFLECTION

What does Rust say to you? Rust indicates that something greater than us is coming up from the earth and into our hearts through Spirit. Rust protects us from difficult circumstances and only allows what will support us into our second chakra. Today, consider the times you've been upset about a loss, or about not having received what you desired, when in fact having this thing wouldn't have been for your highest good. By doing so, you'll see the energy of Rust at work.

WEDNESDAY
JOURNAL JOURNEY

Find your inspiration: Pure and simple, a roadblock has appeared. Whether in your career or elsewhere, you're at an impasse. Struggling on is futile; you'll only reach a dead end.

Reggie Rust protects us from our will, which doesn't always want the best for us. Reggie Rust serves an important purpose. He reminds us that our path is guided and that our current route may be harmful to us. Reggie Rust protects us. Be grateful he's there and remember that there's a plan. If you trust and surrender, clarity will come. Observe yourself emotionally as you allow yourself to be in the place of not knowing.

Today, take some time to journal about how you handle delays. What do you do when you're faced with frustration? Have you learned any tools for dealing with it? Do you just accept it if you feel you're being refused your dreams? Consider how you can move through frustration, surrender to the idea that there may be another path for you and step into emotional maturity.

THURSDAY
MAKE A CONNECTION

Connecting with yourself and others: In the solo exercise, you're going to take off on a journey into the future, where you'll learn what you've accomplished already. This exercise allows you the opportunity to experience the power created when you step into emotional strength. In the group exercise, you'll share tools for helping you to move through impasses and deal with emotional challenges.

Solo exercise: Record your spoken words during this exercise or write notes afterwards. Close your eyes and imagine a train ticket in your hand. You board the train. As it pulls away from the station, the conductor announces that your journey into the future has begun. Look out the window and describe aloud what you see. Someone on the train (a person you know or a stranger) approaches. They tell you about a recent accomplishment of yours. What is it? This person supports your vision of your future and tells you about it as if it's happening now. Repeat what they say. Now another person recognizes you and again begins to tell you all about your future life (to them it's the present). Something in which you'll be involved is impacting this person for the better. Be vocal and say in detail who this person is and how what you do helps them. Three more people come to you and tell you something about your future; the one you've yet to create. As the train brings you back to the present, disembark knowing that your future is secure.

Group exercise: Who in the group does the Reggie Rust story resonate with most strongly? Give them two minutes to share their responses, then allow everyone in the circle a few minutes to write down the tools they use to get "unstuck". Take turns sharing how to handle impasses. Are there similarities in the methods group members use? Returning to the person who originally connected most with Reggie, where are they now? Do they have a belief that needs to be changed? Discuss.

FRIDAY

MEDITATION MEANING

Going within: Remember that your dreams are *not* blocked, even if the way forward isn't obvious. Meditate on the highest outcome for your emotional health. A new route will appear and a new root will be formed to ground you emotionally.

MEDITATION

Visualize that which you wish to create. See yourself doing the very thing that you feel is currently blocked. Allow yourself to experience the joy this outcome will create for you. When you're ready, open your eyes and write down what you have visualized. Remember that there are many paths to your destination.

PERSEVERANCE

Carrot-coloured Cloak

This Week's Focus: Don't quit before the Miracle.

MESSAGE OF THE WEEK

One of the most powerful gifts we can give ourselves is perseverance. Most people quit just before the miracle, because their emotional pain has grown past their capacity to carry on. This week, let's look at what it will take for you to expand your emotional capacity to include real perseverance.

TORI'S TIP

Each part of this fable builds upon the concept of not quitting before the miracle. It reminds us that our main job is to show up, pay attention and tell the truth. Even so, you may find yourself always giving up at the same point. The discipline is in identifying this emotional pressure to quit simply as a storm that will pass.

MONDAY WEEK 14

THE FABLE OF CARROT-COLOURED CLOAK

Shannon had walked for many moons and her Carrot-coloured Cloak was tattered from carrying the burden of her choices. It had been her choice to work day and night pursuing her dreams. Her parents told her that her efforts were futile, yet she'd persevered.

Shannon's Carrot-coloured Cloak had been a gift from a great stage actress. She'd decided on a career in the theatre when she was still a child and once she received the cloak she rarely took it off. She believed that the cloak was the source of her talent. She always wore it during performances, feeling that it possessed a mighty presence all of its own. Those who had the good fortune to see her work were mesmerized by her performance and never noticed the Carrot-coloured Cloak. But Shannon knew better than anyone that her stage presence came from her special cloak.

Following her path, she didn't have the pleasures that friends with more money, time and security enjoyed. From time to time, Shannon longed for fine dining, late-night drinking and trips to exotic places, but these things were not meant for her at the time.

She did occasionally go to parties and movies. She visited her family. And her "normal" friends envied her life. They thought her very adventurous in her career and often wished they had what it took to do what she did.

One morning, Shannon woke up exhausted. All the previous day she'd been comparing her life to her friends' lives. She came to an important conclusion: she simply didn't want to forge along this road anymore. It was too hard. Just yesterday a part that she'd been so right for (yet another part she was "so right for") had been cast with another actress.

Her Carrot-coloured Cloak no longer appeared so dazzling to her. In frustration she threw it off and prayed to the Great Goddess, for she was deeply discouraged.

The Great Goddess appeared before her and spoke. "There is a reason for everything in the universe, little one. Put your favourite cloak back on. You are to keep going. This is your path. It was chosen for you."

But Shannon had already decided to quit and she permanently cast aside her Carrot-coloured Cloak. Yet just ahead on the path, her miracle was waiting to happen – the career success she'd craved for so long. What she didn't know (and what the Great Goddess couldn't tell her, for the Great Spirits never directly tell mortals their future) was that the actress who got Shannon's "perfect part" would be unable to shoot the film. The role would have been Shannon's.

Shannon lost her faith just as her dream was about to come true. And so another artist, persevering, donned the Carrot-coloured Cloak and found the miracle that would have been Shannon's. She'd quit too soon.

First impressions: While the fable illustrates the outcome of quitting too soon, it also tells us that when things seem darkest, a miracle is often just around the corner. The old adage that it's often darkest before the storm is very relevant to the second chakra and reminds us that an emotional storm can just as easily help us to persevere as to quit. In the fable Shannon longs for what she isn't willing to create. She has allowed her emotions to overpower her dream.

Set your intention for the week: Ask yourself, "Am I willing to create emotional fulfilment?" When we long for something emotionally, what we actually long for is a part of ourselves – it's really emotional satisfaction that's eluding us. This week, set the intention to *be* what you long for.

TUESDAY
COLOUR REFLECTION

What does Carrot say to you? Carrot is the colour of movement and of inspiration. It promotes understanding and clear communication and helps get anything that has stalled back on track. Today, make a resolution to get going again! Tap into your emotional truth to move forward even if you're not energized yet. Inspired by Carrot, spend a few minutes identifying areas in which you've reached an impasse and think about how you can regain momentum.

WEDNESDAY
JOURNAL JOURNEY

Find your inspiration: If the Carrot-coloured Cloak resonates with you today, know that changing your direction at this time isn't wise. We never know where our miracle lies on the path; often it's just beyond the boundary of our faith. You may not see it, but it's ahead.

Remember that we do the work chosen for us by a higher order. The Carrot-coloured Cloak is telling you to stick with it and maintain trust in your destiny. Exciting changes are coming and what you work for will come to fruition. You must press on toward your vision.

So far this week, we've worked with ideas about emotional maturity and perseverance. Now, let's think about being with our feelings and forging ahead no matter what. Have you ever tried to walk in a blustery rainstorm? Your umbrella is blown to pieces, you get soaked from head to toe, but you know you're just a few minutes from home so you keep going. Tapping into that energy, that determination to make it home, take a few minutes to write in your journal about how that resolve can translate into your life. What would real emotional perseverance be like?

THURSDAY
MAKE A CONNECTION

Connecting with yourself and others: Ready for a reality check? Today, notice someone who's given up on their dreams. Become aware of their energy. Afterwards, look in the mirror and observe who is looking back. What energy do you see? Now try one of these two exercises to help you stay on your path.

Solo exercise: What is your present path? Go ahead and write what will happen if you stay on course. What will the outcome of your present path be? What will the outcome be if you change direction? If you don't know, act as if you do and write from your knowing place. With both answers in front of you, which is the best course of action for you at this time? Be open to the idea that your best course of action may be to head in a different direction. Allow yourself to discover during this exercise if your current path needs to be altered.

Group exercise: Each group member should write down something that's discouraging them, placing the worry in a hat. Throw in as many concerns as the group needs to! Then one by one, draw a worry out the hat (if you pick your own, take another one). Try this worry on, then help to diminish it by answering the following questions aloud:

- What is it like to have this worry?
- What advice would you offer anyone in this situation?
- How does it feel to try on another person's shoes?
- Would you prefer this worry or do you want your own back?

FRIDAY

MEDITATION MOMENT

Going within: Before doing today's meditation, think about your support system - the allies who believe in you. You need to welcome supportive people into your world. At this time stay away from people likely to denigrate you or your dreams.

MEDITATION

Imagine packing your dreams in a bag. Begin your journey, even if you can't see a path. After a while you come across a magnificent picnic arranged on a cloak. When you have eaten, you notice that your bag is gone. You have given all that you valued to the Great Spirits. Donning the cloak, you continue until you reach a glass wall. Through the glass you can see your goals. Step through the wall. Your cloak falls to the ground, staying with your past. Let it go. You do not need it anymore.

COMPLETION

Final Sunset

This Week's Focus: A life comes to a spectacular close.

MESSAGE OF THE WEEK

This week we think about the importance of endings. We often look back on events to evaluate them, but it's not often that we pause to get perspective on our own existence, much less consider how we feel about it. Are you emotionally present in all phases of your experience, including endings? Or do you avoid them?

TORI'S TIP

This final week in the second chakra is about understanding the emotional power of poignant moments, even if they're painful. In our lives we often try to avoid pain; consider instead that all you have to do is be with your pain and reframe it. Maybe the treasured moments must include those that we know are over.

MONDAY WEEK 15

THE FABLE OF FINAL SUNSET

He was born a few months before his own father's death. He was raised in an orphanage and never had new boots until he enlisted in the army in 1942. He chose the paratroopers because of the poster - he was lured by the drama of it, along with the extra money every month.

Training was hard for him, his asthma a constant enemy, but he was determined. On 6 June 1944 he jumped into Normandy and took part in the liberation of Sainte Mère Église - the first French town freed from the Nazis by the Allies. In September of that same year, he jumped into Holland during Operation Market Garden, and he also survived to tell the tale of the Battle of the Bulge in the December blizzard of 1944.

He received the Bronze Star for heroism, a Certificate of Merit from General Gavin, and a Purple Heart with an Oak Leaf Cluster.

It was in the Bulge one night during a horrible shelling that he lay in a trench and made the most important decision of his life. He promised himself that if he made it out alive, he'd do what he loved for the rest of his life. He was going to be a stage actor.

Night after night, it was his dreams of the theatre that pulled him away from the dead bodies on the battlefield, often the bodies of men who'd saved his life only moments before.

Years later he'd climb dusty stairs in what appeared to be long-condemned buildings, not only to perform but also to support others as they performed. Anyone who says actors are unreliable never knew him. He offered friendship to many who needed it and his memory lives on in the hearts of those who loved him.

History will remember him as a war hero. He watched from above with the Great Goddess as they buried his body. His only child stood near the grave, left with his memory - a legacy to be proud of. In life he'd often say when pressed, "The real heroes never came home."

The Great Goddess smiled on receiving him to the heavens, "Oh, no my friend," she told him. "You were all heroes; those who came home and those who did not."

He laughed to see so many of his old friends.

The Council of the Great Spirits bowed their heads.

First impressions: Consider that the concept of being a hero is never truly embraced by heroes. They remember the sacrifices and struggles that were necessary for them to perform the duty for which they are remembered. What are your struggles and what will you be remembered for?

Set your intention for the week: This final step in your emotional second chakra can be greatly inspirational if you allow it to be. With the rest of your life lying ahead of you, what emotional risk are you willing to take to be, do, have or create what you desire? What would your life be like if you didn't fear things ending? Take a risk this week by setting an intention to declare complete anything that you feel is lingering and dragging you down emotionally.

TUESDAY

COLOUR REFLECTION

What does Final Sunset say to you?: The colour of Final Sunset blends the fierce power of red with the emotion of orange. Action is implied here, even if you only witness it. It may be that you don't recognize the power of your emotions to help you survive the moment in which they appear. Yet a sunset, whether shared or viewed alone, still has the same meaning: it's a conclusion and a poignant understanding that what came before is no longer.

WEDNESDAY

JOURNAL JOURNEY

Find your inspiration: Final Sunset is a reminder to cherish all the beauty in your life, including endings. While many believe that endings are cause to celebrate - the birth of a child is, after all, the end of a pregnancy - it's vital to allow a poignant moment to honour any feelings that are revealed. If you're drawn to Final Sunset, then the Council of the Great Spirits embraces you and the loss you're aware of at this time.

When we stop to watch a sunset, we recognize the beauty of this conclusion of the day. All things have a completion, including life. Remember that there are many who have sacrificed everything so that we may be here.

Now is the time to think about your journey as being part of the greater scheme of things. What does it mean if you're coming to the end of a long emotional road or simply perhaps a project at work? Too often we look to what is next, to what will happen with the dawn, and so we miss the spectacular finale.

Stay in the now, cry, laugh and reflect. Be with the fullness of your experience.

The bars of a prison cell themselves don't keep us in, it's the spacing of them that confines us. Today, make a list in your journal of the things that you'd like to declare complete to create space in your life for something new to appear. Remember that everything in your past has led you to this moment. What would it be like if just for today you declared it all complete? Allow yourself to journal about that and see what possibilities show up for you. How do you feel?

THURSDAY

MAKE A CONNECTION

Connecting with yourself and others: These exercises begin with the end of the story. Whether you write your own eulogy or choose to lie on your deathbed, what do you discover about yourself by recounting what is most important in your life?

Solo exercise: This exercise is about your legacy. In a few paragraphs, write your eulogy in the voice of someone you'd like to deliver it. You can pick a family member, a celebrity or someone whom you greatly admire. Read this person's speech about you aloud to a close friend. When you've finished, describe how this experience affected you. Why did that person speak about you? Have you fulfilled your legacy yet? What is your part in history?

Group exercise: Lie down on the floor. This is your deathbed and you have 15 minutes to live. You've summoned two people (living or dead) to your bedside to say goodbye. Choose two people from the group to play the roles. Speak to them as they sit next to you. When the time is up, close your eyes for a moment. You're gone. Now take a deep breath and open your eyes.

It isn't over yet! What will you vow to do differently from this day forth? Take a few minutes to share your experience of your deathbed with your group.

FRIDAY

MEDITATION MOMENT

Going within: Today is a day of contemplation. Reflect on the legacy you've been given from those who've gone before. Consider your own legacy and take pride in where you come from and what you're doing now. Tell two people about your ancestry today. In the retelling, what do you learn about yourself?

MEDITATION

Make your favourite drink, sit back and imagine your Final Sunset. Allow all your feelings about endings to come to you, whatever they may be. Do you fear them or rejoice in them? Be with this moment. It is a time of awakening, a time to experience your feelings as they are, undiluted. It is a time to reflect upon the past and to remember history. Do some journalling to find clarity here.

MIRACLE

Sun Sparkler

This Week's Focus: Integrity is what turns on the light.

MESSAGE OF THE WEEK

This week we embark on our seven-week journey through the yellow chakra. Yellow relates to your instinct and your intellect, and in this chakra all the fables reveal an aspect of your thought processes. The fable of Sun Sparkler takes place in a town called Darkville; how appropriate that yellow shines light on our thoughts, whether hidden or known.

TORI'S TIP

Think carefully about how you respond to the concept of miracles. Are you resistant, curious, secretive or responsive? Your reaction will reveal whether you're currently open to a miracle taking place in your own life.

MONDAY WEEK 16

THE FABLE OF SUN SPARKLER

No one really knew how the Sun Sparkler first came to illuminate the town of Darkville. There was a rumour that it came on the heels of old Betty correcting Stan in his store; she'd counted the change he'd given her and it was too much. The folks of Darkville thought that was a pretty stupid thing to do. Even Stan had to agree that he wouldn't have handed back the money.

Immediately following this incident, brilliant light burst from the stump of a dead oak tree in the town square and hovered above it like a giant sparkler. It shot a continuous waterfall of dazzling light into the air and lit up all of Darkville. While the townspeople were bewildered by the sudden brightness, they never questioned it, certain that it had been "borrowed" from somewhere else and would be returned to the proper owner if any questions were asked.

For many years tourists travelled great distances to witness the magical light. The people of Darkville hadn't changed at all since the Sun Sparkler had appeared; they still stole, conned money from one another and avoided paying tax. Many a conversation could be overheard in Darkville about how others are "always out to get you, so you have to get them first."

One day, an enterprising lad called Harmon was giving a group of tourists one of his paid tours of the town. An annoyingly inquisitive child was holding up progress and Harmon only had a few minutes before his next tour was due to begin. As they approached the tour's highlight, the Sun Sparkler itself, the child stopped and demanded to know why it shone so brightly.

Harmon couldn't answer and the child turned to the Sun Sparkler. "I've travelled many miles to see you. Will you tell me about yourself?"

Instantly the light dimmed. The townspeople ran out to see what was going on.

"What have you done to our light?" came the cry.

"It wants to speak to me," the child answered.

The crowd grew unruly. Then the Sun Sparkler brightened and began to speak, silencing everyone. "I shine for all that is good in the world. All things are possible when you're kind to your fellows. Serve others always with your work, be gentle, and all your wishes shall be granted. I will shine as long as there is good in the world."

A frail voice emerged from the crowd. "You're so beautiful."

"I came here because of your integrity," said the Sun Sparkler to the woman named Betty.

The crowd of tourists turned from the miraculous light to Betty. She was soon to be richly rewarded by the town for her goodness. From then on everyone in Darkville started to live anew, with honesty and kindness as their motto. And so goes the story of the Sun Sparkler. It is a miracle that still glows brightly for those who live with integrity.

First impressions: This fable tells us that miracles happen when we're in our highest integrity; when we, like Betty, make a rational decision to do the honourable thing. Elevated thinking affects our emotional state, which empowers us. As we're energetically led through the yellow chakra toward the fourth chakra, the chakra of the heart, we're offered the miracle of health and joy.

Set your intention for the week: This week is all about raising your thought process to a new level. Just thinking of more elevated solutions can change your reality. While you built your foundation in the red chakra and addressed your emotional life in the orange chakra, it's in the yellow chakra that you learn how to choose your solutions. This week, set an intention to make uplifting decisions. Ask yourself: "What can I do that will reflect the highest integrity and inspire others and myself?"

TUESDAY
COLOUR REFLECTION

What does Sun Yellow say to you? This, the brightest and boldest of yellows, sheds light on our thinking process. Sun Yellow is a wonderful energy for brainstorming a new project or clearing away negative thinking about something that must be done. There's a sense here of an ability to clear the air and bring you into a new awareness. Spend a few moments today meditating on this colour. What possibilities does Sun Yellow hold for you?

WEDNESDAY
JOURNAL JOURNEY

Find your inspiration: The Sun Sparkler reminds us all that it's through kindness to others and being of service that we find abundance. Are you living your life as fully as you can? Are you honest and kind to others? Do you hold the door open for someone or let it close in their face?

Be open to any awarenesses that come up. Open yourself to the wonder of simple miracles in your life. Allow yourself to know that you create your own miracles every time you make a decision based on faith and wanting to do the right thing for yourself and others.

Today, explore three questions in your journal (keep it simple):

- Have you ever made a decision that inspired you?
- Have you ever been afraid of an outcome but still made a decision based on faith?
- How can you re-create the memory of inspired decision making to support you when you're faced with hard choices in the future?

THURSDAY
MAKE A CONNECTION

Connecting with yourself and others: All miracles begin with the energetic understanding that we must follow our instinct, yet make decisions based on the highest thoughts. Miracles, like seeds, grow best when planted in well-tended soil. We can decide to expect a miracle and also support others in being open to miracles.

Solo exercise: Create a miracle box by thinking of five to seven things you can do to brighten another person's day. Here are a few simple ideas: listening to a friend, letting another car into your lane during rush hour, picking up litter when you see it. Go ahead and create your own. Write these ideas down on separate pieces of paper and create a miracle box for yourself. Do you see how making these decisions can support you emotionally? When you're feeling stuck or something has upset you, take one miracle out of the box and do it to change your state of mind. You can do this exercise any time you're feeling upset. If you'd like to take some time to journal about this exercise, explore what other things you can do to "keep your light on".

Group exercise: In this exercise, each person in the circle answers the following question: "What miracle would you like to happen?" Write down the miracles on separate pieces of paper and put them all in a hat. Each group member now draws out one miracle and takes it home. During the week, throw light on the miracle in your hand. Share what you've learned at the next meeting.

FRIDAY

MEDITATION MOMENT

Going within: Today you'll receive a message in your contemplative state. Sometimes miracles occur when we're doing the opposite of what we think we should be doing. For example, volunteering when you think you should be looking for a job – I can't tell you how many times I've seen this lead people to the miracle they seek. Don't look for the reward, but instead revel in your alignment with Spirit; self-esteem is the gift. Continue to serve others and your life will prosper beyond your wildest dreams. Sun Sparkler lends magic to integrity and honesty.

MEDITATION

Imagine a warm yellow light pouring down from the heavens. Stand directly under the vibrant energy as it showers over you. Allow all material worries to melt away. Sun Sparkler will speak to you now. When you're finished, return to your normal consciousness and write down what you have heard.

ENLIGHTENMENT

Topaz

This Week's Focus: If I seek peace, I must embrace my fears.

MESSAGE OF THE WEEK

Topaz is a healer who's grown tired and seeks solace. He's aware that he must quiet his mind to allow inspired thought to enter his instinctual understanding. Consider the wisdom of your own thoughts this week. We're all on a path; never forget those who travel behind, for those who travel in front remember you.

TORI'S TIP

Topaz reminds you to give your knowledge away to those who may be in need of it. If you're feeling burned out, look at what needs to be done to remove you from a situation in which you're no longer of service. Interruptions of your thoughts are not necessarily disturbances, they may in fact be the very answer you seek.

MONDAY

WEEK 17

THE FABLE OF TOPAZ

Mighty Topaz spoke: "Not many talk of this place, for it cannot be seen. Yet it's where truth is found and harmony is possible. Are you wondering what this place is?"

He waited and the crowd remained silent.

"It is your mind. *You* decide to be happy. That is how you gain peace."

"But ..." began an elder and Topaz held up his hand. "The moment you use the word 'but' you are not in the moment. 'Now' is all we have."

His robe glistened in the afternoon sun as he stood on his rock. The group was growing larger. "I have no answers that you do not already know inside."

Topaz sighed in dismay at the size of the crowd. His trips to the mountain to seek private counsel with the Great Servant were often interrupted. Someone had seen Topaz start up the mountain and the news had spread like a brush fire. Through the village huts and along the stream the whispers ran: "Topaz is on his way up the mountain."

Now Topaz stood before the villagers, moved to speak to those who sought enlightenment.

"While you seek inner peace, that does not mean that you will always be happy."

"What if the goal is happiness?" asked a tall stranger.

"That cannot be a goal," Topaz replied.

"Why not?" the stranger challenged.

"No more than sadness can be a goal," continued Topaz, "For happiness is a feeling. Life is meant to offer challenges and to be difficult at times, like a great puzzle. The only real goal is to be at peace, which in essence is being of service. That is enlightenment. And now it is time that I must leave you."

"Wait!" shouted a small child. "I want to know how to find enlightenment!"

"A noble quest indeed," Topaz agreed as he rose to his feet. "You will gain enlightenment in knowing that there is no one you can change but yourself, in doing what gives you joy so that you may pass it on, and in staying always on the path of peace."

Topaz bade the villagers farewell and set off uphill again.

"Where is the path?" said the youngster trailing after him, "If enlightenment is in my mind, how do I get there?"

The moment before he disappeared into the mist, Topaz replied. "Through your fears."

First impressions: In the most simplistic way, Topaz lays out a formula for enlightenment. Is there a truth in this for you today? Can you decide right now to be happy knowing that the goal is never happiness, but serenity? Understand that the path you seek is the one you're already on.

Set your intention for the week: Though our thoughts may seek happiness, the soul seeks serenity. If you consider that you're always getting the answers to the questions you ask, then the answers you hear may not be what you think they should be. This week, keep your emotions in check and remember that there was a time when you sought information that was generously given to you. Set an intention to be the person that in turn gives knowledge to someone in need. This may lead you exactly where you need to be.

TUESDAY
COLOUR REFLECTION

What does Topaz say to you? Interestingly, the colour Topaz is, like Amber, in constant motion. However, while Amber is ruled by emotion, Topaz represents our ever-changing thought patterns. Because Topaz can appear as the earth energy of brown, the clear intellect of yellow or the magic of gold, it may be that all these qualities apply to it at any given moment. In order to comprehend how the colour affects us we must be able to decipher which aspect of our mind is at play. Today and all this week, think carefully about how you approach interruptions and ask yourself if you're willing to use the knowledge of these observations in your life.

WEDNESDAY
JOURNAL JOURNEY

Find your inspiration: As in all the fables of the third chakra, which vibrate through the colour yellow, we must work here with the concept that conflicting thoughts can both be true. (You'll notice that conflicting thoughts are represented in each of the yellow fables.)

Topaz reminds us that in order to find peace, we must face the fear in our hearts. Because the third chakra lies between the second chakra of emotion and the fourth chakra of the heart, you may find yourself trying to control mentally whatever you feel is out of control.

One of the most powerful tools that can emerge in the third chakra, where it may feel misplaced, is that of prayer or meditation. When your mind runs independently of your true nature it can cause your emotions to flare up in unhelpful ways. In order to practise the principles of mental focus that lead to enlightenment, understand that the mind can offer an illusion like an oasis in the desert. When you remember that your mind is trained to support you in avoiding what will hurt you, you'll understand that your thoughts and your mind can be turned toward a higher understanding.

Pull out your journal and begin to look at the conflicting ideas in Topaz. For example, think about what you dismiss as unimportant and what you place importance on. Make lists, then journal on what this says about you.

Notice how your mind makes meaning out of information. Are there any surprises?

THURSDAY

MAKE A CONNECTION

Connecting with yourself and others: Today's exercises are similar to each other. They each ask you to think about your three greatest gifts and how these have helped you and others. In the solo exercise you reach out for information, while in the group exercise you create a joint plan that becomes the blueprint for your common goals.

Solo exercise: Mighty Topaz has given three gifts to you. What are they? Write down what comes to mind. Now contact three of your closest friends and ask them what *they* think your greatest gifts are. What do you learn?

Group exercise: Mighty Topaz has delivered three gifts to your group. What are they? How can each of you benefit from them? Take turns to share why you think Topaz chose your group to receive these gifts. From this information create a community plan and set an intention for all your lives.

FRIDAY

MEDITATION MOMENT

Going within: In this meditation, you imagine yourself writing down your fears and giving them to Topaz. Are your fears friends, even allies? What will it take for you to step into enlightenment and let your old "friends" go?

MEDITATION

Write down three fears, then close your eyes. In your imagination, hand your list to Topaz as he sits before you. Envision these fears staying with you always. Then visualize them, one by one, walking in faith alongside you. Stride through the Garden of Fear and allow them to stay behind. What is more painful, keeping your fears or releasing them? Be the observer. Notice what you decide; take no action here.

JOY

Dancin' Daisy

This Week's Focus: Let's just jump and see what happens.

MESSAGE OF THE WEEK

This week brings us to joy. Dancin' Daisy is a contagious energy of joy and gratitude, but many people want to smother their own good feelings. We never really get to know Daisy, do we? What we see is the response to her – and to joy itself. This week, we'll look at how your thought patterns expand your joy or try to minimize it.

TORI'S TIP

This fable is about the way we mentally process happiness. How we respond to an issue *is* the issue. Try to observe your thought processes. Are you someone who accepts things at face value? Or are you someone who must rip apart whatever is offered to you in order to understand it and feel safe?

MONDAY WEEK 18

THE FABLE OF DANCIN' DAISY

First time I ever saw Dancin' Daisy I was stopped at a light and she leaped out to cross the street. Well I'll tell ya, I thought she was an angel or somethin', she shined so bright. Could hardly believe my eyes. I was drivin' my old Rambler at the time. I was always gettin' those windshield wipers repaired. When it rained, I couldn't see worth a ... you know.

A few hours later, she was sittin' in my chair and I was trimmin' her hair. She was glowin' when she walked in, said, "This is so exciting, I've never had my hair cut before!"

I said "I can tell," and she laughed. That was her, she laughed about everythin'. When she sat down I felt a kinda joy, damned if I knew why. Didn't have a dern thing to be happy about.

When I touched her hair, I tell you what, I felt all tingly - don't go tellin' my wife, it wasn't like you think. It was like when I was a kid. My Pa ran a store here in town and all us kids would go over there every day for ice cream. Those were fun times, and... Huh? Oh, yeah, the Daisy.

Well, I kept a little of her hair, I put it here in the drawer. I'll get it for you. I didn't really style her hair, just a trim. Here. Now just hold it in your hand. Feel different, don't ya?

My life changed, I tell you. My back didn't ache no more. Tess, that's my wife, thought I was having an affair when I started bringin' home flowers to her. Yep, since that day I cut the Daisy's hair, I feel like a new man.

I'm not the only one who feels this way you know. Rick over at the bank hasn't stopped smiling. Jean, over at the women's store across the square here, says her arthritis has gone away.

Then last week Sid and Fred smashed their cars right into each other. Went to blows over it. Those two have been arguing for years anyhow. When the Daisy appeared out of nowhere, everyone stopped shouting. You got to understand that you just can't shout around her. Sid and Fred stopped fightin' and started discussin' this thing - workin' it out I tell ya. Sid even apologized!

The town's been buzzin' about Dancin' Daisy. Sally, Sid's kid, said Daisy played with her and all she'd say about herself was "I have fun. I love life. It's all joy".

We don't rightly know much about her. We're worried about her, though. No one's seen her since you people came in with your big news cameras to interview her.

Sure is a shame that no one can just be happy, that we have to tear happiness apart figuring it out. I'm glad she was here, but I understand why she's gone. I knew we wouldn't have her here for long. She left the way she came. Peacefully.

First impressions: Most people get very excited when they read this fable. They feel that they're Daisy and are ready to expand and step into their joy. But do we know if Daisy ever experiences joy herself? What if she's actually very sad? What if her story is really about how people use their intellect to pull apart something that could be magnificent? Few people truly experience joy and if they witness it in someone else they may want to take it away, not out of spite but because they're trying to understand it. Daisy reminds us that joy is something we experience and understanding it does not create the feeling.

Set your intention for the week: Trying to understand an emotion from the outside never works. To comprehend a feeling we must experience it. This week, set an intention to be the observer of what brings you joy. Take at least one moment each day to remember what joy feels like. It could be something as simple as seeing your child laugh, playing with your dog, going for a walk, watching a movie or having empowered thoughts.

TUESDAY

COLOUR REFLECTION

What does Dancin' Daisy say to you? Dancin' Daisy combines yellow, the radiating energy of things manifested in the world, with orange, which represents movement. Dancin' Daisy is the harmony that exists when our emotions support clear, unbiased thinking. Today, let's experience how powerful the alignment of your thoughts with your emotions really is. Stay in the joy of Dancin' Daisy and imagine radiating this balance of colour and energy out into the world. Look for small miracles. When today is over, take stock of what has occurred.

WEDNESDAY

JOURNAL JOURNEY

Find your inspiration: Dancin' Daisy represents an acceleration of events and the start of a new chapter in your life. Dancin' Daisy says, "Come to me and jump beyond what you believe, into a new possibility." She tells you to take action where you may not have dared previously.

Dancin' Daisy is a gift. She's energy, enthusiasm and expansion. She embodies in physical form an example for us all. She represents a joyous time for you and an important change in your life – a move, a new job or a marriage. Keep the faith and take a risk. It will work out.

Dancin' Daisy also represents radiant health. The Great Spirits can only manifest through us if we honour the physical body we inhabit. This may mean that you need to adopt a fitness programme. Your will to heal yourself is great.

If a man is particularly attracted to this fable, that's a clear indication that he's pulling a new partner into his life. This could be a life partner or some other strong female energy. It's also an indication that he should look to a woman for his next brilliant idea.

If a woman is specially attracted to this fable, she should know she's a radiant being attracting all that she needs.

Today, consider what doors enthusiasm could open for you. In your journal, take some time to explore how you've changed the circumstances of your life simply by changing your attitude. If at any moment you could tap into the vital energy of Dancin' Daisy to create magic in your life, what would that experience be like? How would your life change?

THURSDAY

MAKE A CONNECTION

Connecting with yourself and others: These two very different exercises look at the things that create joy in your life. Get ready to play with your joy.

Solo exercise: What are your joy-makers? Take a few moments to write down the activities that give you joy. Perhaps you like spending time with a favourite friend, listening to music, watching the stars ... Are you regularly doing these things? Make a commitment to yourself do at least one activity on your list each week.

Group exercise: You've been invited on a TV show to discuss your experience of joy. As a group, take a few moments to write down the questions that the show's host is going to ask. Each person then does a five-minute interview, with one group member playing the part of the host. As you speak, be as enthusiastic as Daisy was about her haircut. Afterwards, think what would happen if you took this same enthusiasm into every aspect of your life. How would your world change?

Did you discover anything about yourself doing this exercise? What was the experience like for the person playing the host? Discuss.

FRIDAY

MEDITATION MOMENT

Going within: This meditation is excellent if you're feeling tired or run down. Its regenerative energy is also great for creative visualization.

MEDITATION

Sit with Dancin' Daisy. Look at her and invite joyful energy to fill you. Now imagine a ball of sunshine in your solar plexus. Let it expand, allowing the room to be filled with this radiant energy. Send it out to the universe with love. Things manifest quickly after touching this energy, so create what you desire. Carry this energy forward to everyone you encounter today. Observe the results.

PRAYER

Cool Lemonade

This Week's Focus: My prayers are answered.

MESSAGE OF THE WEEK

This week you determine what an authentic inner voice is and find out if yours is expressed in your present path. Keep asking yourself if you're doing the right work and if you're in alignment with your dreams.

TORI'S TIP

On any journey it's important to take stock of where you've been, in order to gain perspective on your life. Cool Lemonade is a fable of reflection. Take time every day this week to contemplate a beautiful moment.

MONDAY

WEEK 19

THE FABLE OF LEMONADE

Yesterday, I reflected back on the past 68 years. Now, it's not very often I do that, I'm usually too busy living. I was sitting on the porch with my grandson, Greg. We was looking out at the fields that we just finished planting. I don't think either one of us could move. It's nice to think that hard work tires out the young same as the old.

The lemonade was so cool going down. I almost forgot how good it could taste.

Greg said, "Grandpa, what's so funny?"

I glanced at the lad. I guess I'd been laughing about the irony of life. If the good Lord had answered my prayer, Greg wouldn't be here.

I'd wanted so badly to get away from home when I was a boy. I'd wanted to go to the big city and make my dreams come true. I was going to bring peace to the Earth, become a travelling preacher and show others the way.

The day I was all set to leave, my truck broke down. So I didn't go. Once I got the thing all fixed up, the floods came. I prayed for them to stop and they did. But in their wake they left an awful mess. I couldn't leave my folks then, they needed my help.

I prayed to the Lord to make everything OK so I could leave - and He did. My mother won a new suitcase at bingo and we took it as a sign. We packed it up full and I was ready to be on my way first thing in the morning.

My daddy came to me that night and we had the only talk we ever really had. He told me to listen to what the Lord intended, not what I wanted. And he said if I listened for direction, I'd never be upset by where I was pointed.

I still remember him standing in the doorway that night. The last words he ever spoke to me were, "I love you, son." He died in his sleep that night.

I quietly unpacked the next morning. Darn if my black suit wasn't at the bottom of the suitcase. After the funeral, all the relatives were asking when I was leaving. Momma, bless her heart, pulled me into the kitchen and begged me to go.

My daddy would've wanted me to go, she said.

I'd smiled then, the way I would with Greg. I knew the Lord was pointing me in the right direction. I was not meant to teach values to folks who were already heading where they were guided to go.

Sure I've had hard times, who hasn't? But I've never been disappointed by the way my life turned out.

"Grandpa ... you OK?"

"I'm just fine, Greg," I said.

"You didn't tell me why you were smiling."

"Just enjoying the twilight, son."

"This is great lemonade, ain't it Grandpa?"

"Sure is, son. Sure is."

First impressions: What shows up in our life is who we are, not what we ask for. Being guided means living to the highest possible truth, because life doesn't happen to us, it happens through us. There's a gentle reminder in this fable to calm the mind and allow our life to find us.

Set your intention for the week: What would your life be like if your mind could switch to serenity at any moment? The most powerful tool offered here is the ability to reflect with forgiveness and an understanding that you've been guided all along. Today and every day this week, take time to reflect with a peaceful mind and allow your thoughts to support the highest part of you. Think the best of yourself and allow others to do the same for themselves.

TUESDAY

COLOUR REFLECTION

What does Lemonade say to you? Lemonade is a colour of precision; just the right amount of sugar needs to be added to make the sour sweet. This colour reflects your brightness and creativity and has an element of sweetness. It offers an ability to see the details and correct imperfections without judgment. Lemonade is cool and decisive; it reflects the power of making a decision. Today and all this week, if you're feeling off-track, Lemonade reminds you to cool your thoughts, allow yourself to be serene and open yourself to Spirit's guidance to bring you back into alignment with your desires.

WEDNESDAY

JOURNAL JOURNEY

Find your inspiration: Chasing dreams can leave us winded and unhappy, but remember that there's always a plan. If you've been sidetracked from your proper path, you'll be guided back to it. There's not always a complicated reason why things don't work out the way you'd like them to. Each of us has a spiritual path. Knowing that is the magic of Cool Lemonade.

Are you sure your prayers weren't answered? Or did you refuse to hear the reply? You'll find peace when you accept the gifts you have, rather than pining for those you lack. Pray and ask the Great Spirits to show you the many gifts they've already given you. The point of prayer isn't to get what we want, but to ask to be of service. Cool Lemonade reminds us to seek to be of service.

Your goals are closer than you think and could be simpler than you imagine. Stop and take a break before proceeding.

Today, write a letter to your wise older self who sits on the porch sipping lemonade. What are you happy your future self accomplished for you? Can you adopt any of these insights to help transform your life now?

THURSDAY

MAKE A CONNECTION

Connecting with yourself and others: Gratitude and enthusiasm help you reach your goals. These two exercises encourage you to look back at your journey so far. By reminding yourself which of your dreams have already come true, you'll empower yourself to plan your direction knowing you can succeed.

Solo exercise: Are there things in your life that you wanted to have, do or be that did not happen? As you look back now, can you see why they didn't happen? What were the blessings in this? Make a list. Are any of these items things that you still desire today? Be bold and declare what it is you've learned that has cleared the way for your dreams now to become reality. Be open to sharing your learning with another person and see what they have to say regarding your ideas.

Group exercise: Write down three things that today are in your life that were, at one time, only something you dreamed about. Choose one or all of them to share with your group. Discuss the process of their creation with the group - how you manifested these things. Now write down three new things that you'd love to have in your life. Could you manifest them too? Ask the group to support you as you make these things happen.

FRIDAY

MEDITATION MEANING

Going within: In today's meditation we connect with what makes us happy. The key here is that we must only pray to be of service. Spirit knows what you desire. Finding happiness within will attract your desires to you.

MEDITATION

Knowing that you cannot take anything with you when you leave the Earth, that thoughts create your world, think now of the things that make you happy. Having all that you desire begins with taking what you need at the right time. Trust that you will be offered the best. Whether or not you take what is offered is entirely up to you.

DISSIPATING

Canary Yellow

This Week's Focus: I am more than I think I am.

MESSAGE OF THE WEEK

This week, we work with the mental discipline necessary to channel our energy into creativity. In this way we can learn to direct our mental energy and use it for the greater good.

TORI'S TIP

While Canary Yellow is a reminder that wasted energy is gone for ever, this fable is also about the dangers of bravado. Are you being authentic in your conversations? It's enough to enjoy the journey without constantly talking up what you're doing. The power of focused intention will come to the forefront this week.

MONDAY WEEK 20

THE FABLE OF CANARY YELLOW

Once upon a time, there was a canary named, well, Canary. He was quite petite, but very proud. Canary was pure yellow and unafraid to speak up. In fact he spoke to anyone who'd listen.

He chirped often about the screenplay he had in mind. Canary loved watching action films with Mrs Robinson, his owner, who herself had been at one time a famous actress. She'd appeared in too many films to count. If you looked in the crowd, you'd see her.

Canary knew they were kindred spirits for Mrs Robinson, like him, didn't need to speak to be a star. Although she'd point out her presence to him when they watched films, he of course recognized her without help. She'd praise Canary as her hero, and he in turn spoke often of the film he was writing for her. They were a happy pair. When they had company, Mrs Robinson allowed Canary to entertain her friends by telling them about the script he was working on. He'd expound for hours, explaining every nuance of his plot and characters.

The film was about a canary who saved the world and his lady friend who saw the greatness in him, allowing him to shine.

They continued to live in this way for many years, until one day Mrs Robinson's daughter gave Canary some money to buy a computer. She'd become so convinced of his talents that she decided he needed the proper device to record this wonderful story. She gave her mother more money to hire someone to work with Canary on the screenplay.

But alas, as is the case with many stories, Canary's screenplay was never actually written. Indeed, when presented with everything they needed, Mrs Robinson and Canary took the money and embarked on a world cruise.

They spent their days delighting others with tales of the screenplay they were working on. Once, a fellow passenger - a scriptwriter - offered to finish the story for them, but Canary and Mrs Robinson were both insulted by this offer that meant they'd have to give up creative control. No. This was to be *their* story. And so it was. Their story - a story never written.

First impressions: Canary is full of big ideas and loves to chatter on about things that he'll never actually do. Here we become aware of the power of the spoken word. If all our communication is either an offer of love or a plea for help, do you see both in Canary? Are you able to see what your words are - a plea or an offer?

Set your intention for the week: Think about the word "dissipating". We define this as "causing to disappear". Overthinking leads to mental exhaustion and going on too long with our story causes others to lose interest. This week, set an intention to be aware of the ways in which your thinking exhausts you. What aspect of your life drains you? Is it a person? A place? An element of your job? Be in inquiry. Allow yourself to see the thoughts you entertain that drain your energy.

TUESDAY

COLOUR REFLECTION

What does Canary say to you? Yellow in its purest form, Canary is intellectual. It thinks and configures what makes sense. The planner in you resides in Canary. Here things are boldly communicated and plans are well orchestrated. Beware, however, of the perpetual plan and lack of doing. Canary brings creativity that must be freed from its cage. This yellow can overcommit and have difficulty moving into the doing. Today, take the first step to set a plan in motion.

WEDNESDAY

JOURNAL JOURNEY

Find your inspiration: Canary suggests that you open your eyes to see what really *is*. What you're doing now may not be your true calling and you may need to move beyond what you currently believe to be acceptable. Would you rather carry on living in a fantasy? This is your opportunity to do it or let it go. Others will soon see what you're either hiding or denying. Time to wake up or you may find yourself embarrassed when your true motive is revealed. Remember Canary, who would rather impress than do.

This fable also denotes the person who works too much and neglects the reality of their life. This person feels that they'll never receive what they're entitled to, so it's preferable to pretend that everything is fine.

Canary indicates that circumstances are ready for the miracle to take place, but it may not if you dissipate your energy. Often we're limited by the story we tell about what we're doing. Don't take yourself or the project you speak of so seriously any longer. Stop and consider whether you intend doing what you say - or whether you're only talking for the sake of talking.

This is the fable of realizing that we own nothing. Even inspiration comes to us from above. If we dissipate our gifts, then we don't fulfil our promise to Spirit. If you resist using your voice, why have one at all?

As you step into the energy of Canary Yellow, make some time today to write down in your journal the ways in which you avoid doing what you say you want to do. Can you get clear about how you dissipate your energy?

THURSDAY

MAKE A CONNECTION

Connecting with yourself and others: "What if?" is a powerful query. These two exercises consider a "what if" that has been pending for a long time. Set your plan in motion. If not now, when?

Solo exercise: Is there something that you think you could do or could have done, if you "really wanted to"? In this exercise, we're going to explore the idea of delay or indecision. Take a few moments to write down something you've been promising yourself to do for a while. Now ask yourself: "Do I really want to do this? Or is this something that's taking me away from my true gifts?" If you decide that you do want to do this particular thing, go inside and allow your mind to wander to a calendar hanging on a wall. Imagine flipping through the calendar until you find a month that calls to you - perhaps you'll even notice the specific date. Then open your eyes and make some notes about what it would take for you to do what you'd like to by this date.

Group exercise: Is there someone who you have unfinished business with? Are you collaborating in someone else's limitations? Or is someone else collaborating in your limitations? Get another group member to play the other person. Admit your part in the "game" with this other person and agree to be authentic. When all group members have taken part, discuss what happened.

FRIDAY

MEDITATION MEANING

Going within: Is it money that makes you happy or dancing in the rain? Is it being in the arms of the person you love? This meditation will help you to create anything you wish for. Trust that when the time is right, you'll be offered the best of the best. Taking what's offered is entirely up to you. Just be mindful that having all that you desire begins with taking what you need at the right time.

MEDITATION

Sit quietly with what you speak of so frequently. Take a breath. What do you wish to do? Become aware of the feeling in your body. Is it apprehension? Enthusiasm? In your mind's eye, take one step toward carrying out your wish. For example, are you thinking of writing a book? Pull out the first sheet of paper or turn on the computer. Then take the next step. Then the next. Will you dream it - or do it?

FAÇADE

Bronze God

This Week's Focus: This isn't who I am.

MESSAGE OF THE WEEK

A façade is a false front, one we show the world for appearance's sake. This week, we'll look at the path of rediscovering your authentic voice and of reclaiming the past to integrate it into your life in a way that empowers you.

TORI'S TIP

We all have a lost child within us, but this fable strikes a chord especially for survivors of deep wounding in childhood. We may put up a façade to protect ourselves and appear normal, but this requires us to play a role that drains our life-energy. To free ourselves from whatever it is that chains us to the past, we must appreciate the survival skills that carried us through our previous difficulties.

MONDAY WEEK 21

THE FABLE OF BRONZE GOD

There once was a bronze boy named Darnel, who had to become the man of the family at a young age when his father passed away. Darnel was sensitive and caring, but as he grew he had to be strong and brave for the people in his life. During his formative years, his family needed him to be there for each of them. He secretly enjoyed the respect he got and basked in the power that came from his position in the family. One day he met a bronze goddess named Kerry. He knew instantly that she was the one for him. She looked up to him much like his family did and he was strong for her. He was her hero. They fell in love and soon married.

When their first child, Evan, was born, Darnel provided for Kerry and their newborn. He loved his tiny son and wanted for Evan the freedom to be a child that he'd never had.

Quite unexpectedly, Darnel lost his livelihood. His world began to unravel.

He went to his mother for help, but she was too busy with her own problems. His sisters offered no help. "You'll pull through," they assured him. "Apply yourself to the task at hand. Do for others to get your self-esteem back. That's what you always told us ..."

Kerry was pregnant again. She was too preoccupied with keeping the family going to listen to Darnel. He needed someone to understand. Anyone. He decided to take a walk to clear his head. When he reached the park he stopped to watch the children playing. His sisters had played here many times, but he never had. There'd been too many things to do.

Darnel slid down behind a tree and cried. He'd never sat on the grass in a park before! He tried to wipe away his tears, but more came. They wouldn't stop! Soon he was sobbing like a baby and the people nearby were staring at him. He tried to hush himself but was unable to, and this frightened him. This child was too loud and Darnel pushed the tiny spirit away. He couldn't do this. He closed his eyes and fell into a deep sleep called life.

Many years later he awoke a grandparent. This was when he met his two grown children – the ones he'd raised but never knew.

One night when the family was playing games, Evan's son, Hayven, knocked over the board. Everyone laughed. Everyone except Darnel. He thought Hayven had been stupid and clumsy. Kerry reminded her husband that little Hayven was only three years old.

Darnel watched the small child as he hid behind his grandmother's chair, fearful of his grandfather's anger. Darnel recognized the little boy inside him who'd been hiding too, all these years. Darnel approached his son with his head hung low. He was sorry. Evan stood and faced his father. Darnel's eyes flooded with the love he'd never known how to show his own son. They embraced and Hayven joined in.

Before his death, Darnel came to understand that it was on that day in the park that his life had been charted. He'd ignored all the children in his life, beginning with the one inside. As he left the Earth plane, he paused at the park to pick up the child who was still crouched behind a tree.

The child had been there waiting all these years. This time, Darnel took the small hand and together they walked into the clouds.

First impressions: Are you presently caught up in a life that you're not happy with? Now that you've read the fable, take time to decide if this is still your choice. Consider the responsibility of owning your choices. Hint: anything you choose can be changed - and we choose everything.

Set your intention for the week: The Bronze God reminds us that it's our responsibility to be true to ourselves. This week, consider who you hold accountable for the person you've chosen to be. It's not anyone else's fault if you invited others to rely upon you and they've come to do so. Set an intention to be honest about your own feelings. Consider what it would be like to be exactly who you are. Remember, we only hide from ourselves.

TUESDAY
COLOUR REFLECTION

What does Bronze say to you? The colour of Bronze carries the message of earthly values and this is what ruled Darnel. The metallic quality is what adds rigidity to Darnel's choices. Bronze is about wealth and will expose anything that is not authentic. Use it wisely. Bronze is also all about being grounded. A permanence is implied here. Today, think back to a time when you decided to give up a part of you for the good of others. Remember that your choice was noble, yet today decide to reclaim the part that you once gave away.

WEDNESDAY
JOURNAL JOURNEY

Find your inspiration: Be careful not to blame others for the way you've chosen to be. Are you being honest about who you are? Are you thinking that you have to pretend to be something that you're not? Bronze God reminds you that you may be hiding something from yourself that could hurt you. Your relationships with others will not be successful if you take up a role that's not authentic.

Are you taking on too much responsibility in your life? You may need to go out and play. Exercise, go to a movie, take your family on a picnic. Don't be so serious about yourself or your work. If you crush your need to play, you may lose all your creativity. Take a break, relax and get back in touch with your playful self.

In your journal ask yourself the following questions:

- Are people responding to me in a way that makes me feel fully actualized and heard?
- Do I feel that people are responding to someone other than me, almost as if I'm invisible?
- Am I presenting my most authentic self to others? Why (or why not)?

THURSDAY

MAKE A CONNECTION

Connecting with yourself and others: These exercises encourage you to see your authentic self, by connecting you with your playful side and asking you to imagine a "photo album of truth" that shows you exactly as you are. After you've done your chosen exercise, try to take on tasks in a light-hearted manner and have fun, without being overwhelmed by your work. Always remember who you really are.

Solo exercise: The true freedom of play will break down any façade. So play! Write down the name of one person you've been meaning to play with. Set an intention to contact that person and make a play date. Have fun!

Group exercise: In your group, imagine that all the members have been handed a photo album of truth. Inside are pictures of how others see you. Open the album. Point out at least five of the imaginary snapshots and describe to your group the quality in you that has been captured on paper for others to see. Discuss as a group. Take it in turns for each group member to do the same.

FRIDAY

MEDITATION MOMENT

Going within: This meditation involves flying around the room! By experiencing it, you can connect to that part of you that's in a constant state of joy. Bronze God needs you to play.

MEDITATION

Imagine yourself as a child, running and taking flight. Veer off to the clouds and find a playground in the sky. Swing, slide, laugh and, if you choose, find other children to play with. Enjoy yourself. While you are there, you will receive a message of some kind. You can ask your child-self if there is anything you need to know.

ABUNDANCE

Gold Coins

This Week's Focus: I only seek to give you what you ask for.

MESSAGE OF THE WEEK

This week we look at your relationship with money and consider the profound changes involved in creating true internal abundance. We also look at how two conflicting thoughts may both be true – and yet we allow this to keep us stuck. By exploring the reality of your financial situation, you can begin to see what's going on in your underlying thought processes.

TORI'S TIP

Interestingly, this is the only fable directly related to money. It's an opportunity to think about your financial beliefs. Remember, beliefs are fear-based – not faith-based. Be observant this week regarding your thoughts and beliefs about money.

MONDAY WEEK 22

THE FABLE OF GOLD COINS

This is the story of the Gold Coins, huddled together in a large treasure chest. After all, that's where Gold Coins can congregate alone, without suspicion. They're waiting, untouched. Waiting to be found by someone.

The coins frequently talk among themselves. Let's listen:

"Those humans," a square coin said, "They're a scream! All they do is wish for me, then they don't know what to do with me once they get me!"

"Know what you mean," echoed a smaller coin. "One guy was so nervous about having me, he dropped me into a drain."

Laughter rolled out from the chest.

"Excuse me," said an especially shiny coin. "What happened to the guy that lost you?"

"I don't know." The small coin replied.

A tarnished old coin coughed. "Didn't he try to get you back?"

"Well, he cried over me for a long time before he went away."

"How'd you get out?" the shiny coin asked.

"Well," replied the small coin, "funny thing about it, I sat down there for the longest time, until one day a little girl came along with a piece of string and chewing gum. I could hear people laughing at her. She'd seen me down there and believed I could be hers."

A coin chuckled. "Then what are you doing with us, wise guy?"

"Oh, she saved me up with many others and after many years she used me to buy her first house."

The tarnished oldster dabbed his eyes. "That's a lovely story."

Copper, the group intellectual, threw in his money's worth. "Yes, well isn't it every coin's dream to be well spent?"

The crowd sighed in agreement.

First impressions: There are many different perspectives on money. Can you see your own in this fable? "Currency" also means "circulation". That means that money has to flow. Are you in flow? Be aware that great riches are waiting for you to use them. You can ask the universe for great riches or great poverty; the universe doesn't care. Only you can change your inner knowledge.

Set your intention for the week: This week, as you consider the idea of being wise (or foolish) with money, continually ask yourself this question: "What is it that I want from money?" Too often, we think we want money but we don't know what to do with it. This week set an intention to have a knowing about money. In other words, ask yourself "What will I do with all that money that I'm going to create?"

TUESDAY
COLOUR REFLECTION

What does Gold say to you? Since Gold is the essence of yellow, it has a strong connection to intellect. This is the colour that says, "I can receive abundance. Trust me to get things done." Think today about the decisions you've already made about money. Does it serve you? If you don't like rich people it will be hard to become one, for you'll never become what you resent. Today, find someone who is financially successful and ask them about their attitude toward money.

WEDNESDAY
JOURNAL JOURNEY

Find your inspiration: The Gold Coins gently ask you to look at your relationship with money. Which character do you identify with most – the man who loses his money or the girl who finds it? Are you blaming something on money? Be wary of using your financial situation as an excuse.

Is there any difference between seeking to be closer to the Great Spirits and receiving financial riches? Wealth is wealth, whether spiritual or material. Are you using money issues to question a relationship or career that's hitting a rocky time? It may be time to look for the good in it. Remember, there are two sides to every coin.

How are you at receiving? This will tell you how you are with money. Money is drawn to gratitude. If you're gracious and enthusiastic all you need to do is expand that energy around money. Money journeys everywhere but stays where it's welcome.

Today, journal regarding your thoughts about money. How have you interpreted the material so far this week? If you've been in any way upset, acknowledge it and write down your experience. Remember, if we don't have money it's simply because we haven't created the container to hold it. Journal about the container you're currently creating.

THURSDAY
MAKE A CONNECTION

Connecting with yourself and others: We all play games with money. What's your game? To shift your consciousness consider playing one or all of the games here. If one of these games resonates specially with you, what does that reveal?

Solo exercise: Write down an amount of money that you'd like to attract on a card. You must have a strong reason for creating this money – in your mind, be specific about your reason. Put the card somewhere where you can see it every day. Meditate, imagining the powerful energy of money that you've generated swirling around you, flowing out into the universe. Call it your "money energy". As you send out this energy to the universe, trust that money will attach to it and come to you.

Alternatively, pick a magic word. Don't make it too obscure. The first time I did this I picked the word "time". Each *time* I heard the word, I knew the universe was sending me money. It was really fun! As soon as you can after you've picked your word, give a coin to a stranger. It doesn't have to be someone in dire straights. Just tell a stranger you'd like to give money. Once you send the coin out to the world the magic will begin. Now, each time you hear the word, money is on its way to you. Ask the universe to bring it to you.

Group exercise: Have each member bring a new coin or paper note to the group (all coins/notes should be of the same value). The money mustn't be borrowed. Each member should energize the money by saying aloud, "I send energy into this money. I endow it with the gift of attraction. As long as I release it with love, it will attract thousands of friends to me." Now pass it to the person on the right, until everyone in the circle has touched the money. Carry this money with you for one week, then lovingly give it away. Watch how it attracts friends.

Alternatively, take a moment to recall your first memory about money. How has this shaped your belief about money today? Share these thoughts with your team. Are the beliefs empowering? Great! Or disempowering? If so, with the team's energy, come up with a few new ideas that will create a new story about money.

FRIDAY

MEDITATION MOMENT

Going within: When you do your meditation notice the energy of money. Do you feel anything? What if anything do you observe?

MEDITATION

Place some money before you. Pick it up. Have you thought about how many souls have touched it before it came to you? Feel its energy. The value we derive from money is the exchange of energy. Ask now for what you desire. Imagine this money transforming into your desire. Be aware of your improved relationship with money. Be aware of your personal abundance.

FROM THE LOWER TO THE HIGHER CHAKRAS

Integrating the Red, Orange and Yellow Chakras

MESSAGE OF THE WEEK

Welcome to the higher chakras! This week we're going to look at integrating what you've learned so far in the red, orange and yellow chakras, and also at what you can expect in the green, blue, purple and neutral chakras. You're going to practise using your intuition, before you step into your heart.

TORI'S TIP

By now you'll have realized that the path you're taking through the chakras is a deeply personal one. This week is a chance to see how serendipity plays into your life. As coincidence is your angels' way of acting anonymously, the exercises this week will confirm for you that your intuition is powerful.

MONDAY WEEK 23

LOOKING BACK AND FORWARD

Let's recap the value of the first three chakras before you move on to the green chakra and start exploring what's true to your heart. Your red chakra reveals what you create in this life. With a solid red chakra you bring into being or fruition the magic you're here to work. Nothing is created in the seventh chakra. You create in the first chakra (red), you're supported emotionally in the second chakra (orange) and you begin your plan of action in the third chakra (yellow). Therefore, these first three chakras provide the foundation of your ability to manifest and create your life.

This week we're working with the concept of the dawn – the second aspect of your awakening. Now is your chance to integrate in a very individual way what you've learned from the fables of the first three chakras. Much has taken place over the past few months: you've discovered tools to help you build your life; you've looked closely at whether or not you're supporting yourself emotionally and you've gained an understanding of your thinking and planning and gathered tools to help you with these processes.

So what is to come?

The green chakra

In the fourth chakra, you'll balance the solid foundation you've created with your higher consciousness. All seven fables in the green chakra represent an aspect of your heart's desire.

Whether you follow it, ignore it, resent others for having it or hide from it, everything about your heart will emerge here. In this chakra, you admit the truth of your heart, give up what no longer serves you and begin to see the power available to you when you allow your heart to guide you. Note that I'm saying "guide", not "run your life". When people are emotionally unbalanced and say they're controlled by what's in their heart, then they're not acting according to their heart, but according to fear-based instinct. This is an issue that must be resolved in the third chakra. The heart is always about balance. If there's an imbalance, it will usually be found in the third, yellow chakra of our thinking. In that case, we're not following our heart, but being obsessive.

The blue chakra

All the fables in the fifth chakra represent aspects of communication, from verbal to creative to silent. Here we must ask, "Is the message sent the one being received?" Truly, one of the most powerful aspects of the blue fables is the unspoken communication implied in each of them. Consider what messages you're sending out to the world and how you do this energetically without ever uttering a word.

Even silently we're creatures of expression and each of these seven fables gives us powerful tools to work with our own expression in the world. Be mindful as you go through this seven-week section that the blue chakra fables represent how you are in the world. Think about the people you've never met in person but you feel you know very well. We form opinions of famous people often without listening to what they actually say. The blue chakra calls your attention to the response you are getting from the world. Consider this statement: "My outer reality reflects my inner reality."

The purple chakra

The fables of the sixth chakra all represent our sixth sense in one form or another. It's in these fables that we often find hidden (or unresolved) family agreements. One of the important concepts here is that each purple fable represents a family dynamic and as a result unfinished business frequently shows up in this chakra.

Your intuitive gift will also appear during these weeks, giving you the keys not only to your future but also to your profound questions about life. All these fables are related to your intuition and higher consciousness. By tapping into the purple fables you'll activate your own psychic awareness. These fables also represent the concept of personal honour.

The neutral chakra

The final seven fables are housed in the seventh chakra outside our physical body. While the seventh chakra is typically seen as violet, it can also be represented as gold, the brilliant light from heaven. In my work, the seventh chakra is neutral in colour, representing the impartial nature of the universal consciousness. Each of these fables represents universal themes and has a powerful connection with Spirit. You can easily see the highest calling of each story as each one will offer insight for when you're out of spiritual alignment.

The true power of the neutral fables is that they bring support from your spirit guides and allow you to define yourself without outside interference. They also offer purpose and meaning – your very identity resides here.

Set your intention for the week: This week you'll follow your intuition and allow your angels to speak to you as you integrate the lessons you've learned in the red, orange and yellow chakras. Remember what I said about trusting the process? Set your intention for the week to be open to your own inner wisdom.

TUESDAY

COLOUR REFLECTION

What does the red chakra say to you? Pick a number from 2 to 8. Now go to that week in the red chakra. Look at Tuesday's colour reflection. What does this tell you about the foundation you've thus far created with this work? Do you need to take on an aspect of this lesson to strengthen your foundation? What is it about this particular colour that ties into what you've received from your family of origin? What do you notice?

WEDNESDAY

JOURNAL JOURNEY

Find your inspiration: Today, pick a number from 9 to 15 and go to that week in the orange chakra. Read the text of Wednesday's journal journey and take some time to do the journalling task again. This time, be a neutral observer, step back and ask yourself how this particular fable and journal activity are currently impacting your emotional world. Can you see how this perhaps ties into a legacy from your family? You may be reminded of a learned behaviour or of something that has been passed down to you emotionally from your family. Is there an aspect of your understanding that you need to deepen here? Is there a new perspective on your emotional life that you may need to take on in order to live the truth of your heart?

THURSDAY

MAKE A CONNECTION

Connecting with yourself and others: Today, pick a number from 16 to 22 and go to that week in the yellow chakra. Now, in the role of neutral observer, look at either the group or solo exercise of the fable you've intuitively picked.

Solo exercise: Ask yourself: "What is it about this solo exercise that relates to me right now? What is it about this thinking process or the way I plan that is either a challenge or a gift for me?" Consider if any of your answers can be traced back to one of your grandparents. What insight does this give you?

Group exercise: Each group member chooses a number from 16 to 22, thus picking a yellow fable. Notice if all the fables are different or if the group has selected the same fable more than once. One by one, each person then stands up, as though they're making a toast at a wedding. Holding their glass high, they propose a toast about how the group exercise belonging to the fable they chose has changed their life. The fun of this exercise is that each member gets a chance to talk about how the exercise affected them and who they are today because of it. After each person has finished, the group applauds the speech. When everyone has taken a turn, discuss your experience as a group.

FRIDAY

MEDITATION MOMENT

Going within: In the next chakra you move on to your heart. Trust that you'll be guided and that what you've learned so far has created a solid foundation for you to open your heart and step into the next stage of your journey.

MEDITATION

Close your eyes and invite the Great Spirits to join you. Ask them to place a number from 1 to 3 in the palm of your hand. Open your eyes. What number have you been given? Now, close your eyes again and ask for another number from 1 to 7. Open your eyes. What number have you been given? The first number indicates the first (red), second (orange) or third (yellow) chakra. The second number indicates which fable you should revisit. Look at the meditation again. Do you notice anything different about it?

VICTIM

Green Acorn

This Week's Focus: I am not a victim! I chose to do what I am doing!

MESSAGE OF THE WEEK

We begin our journey through the heart chakra with a fable that exposes the excuses we give to settle for less. An excuse is always directly related to a belief and all beliefs are based on fear. This week, take on what you know to be true in your heart, because what we know is always based on love.

TORI'S TIP

Acorn represents the stories we tell ourselves that may disempower us. This fable offers us the opportunity to rewrite them. If you think that your life is outside your control, this week is a chance for you to open your heart to a new way of being. If you're looking for that "one thing", this may be the opening you're waiting for.

MONDAY WEEK 24

THE FABLE OF GREEN ACORN

How do you do? I'd like to introduce myself: I was the lovely green acorn who starred in the fable of Kelly the Green Dragon. Although I was originally hired to have a speaking part, my best work never made the final edit. I want to tell you what really happened.

I was told that it was going to be a tale of how an acorn creates a remarkable friendship between two forest creatures. I was honoured to be offered a part like that. But Squirrel and Dragon felt that their parts weren't big enough and the arguing began. It was a nightmare. I was so completely stressed, I lost weight and then they started complaining that I needed to be rounder.

This is what happened. I was sunning myself, having just tumbled off a tree, and was about to roll over to do the other side, when I was tapped on my crown by Dragon (I still have that unsunned pale patch on one side). He said he wanted to make me a star. He'd put me in a fable, with top billing. Was that something I was interested in? Harrumph, of course!

He lied. The fable turned out to be about him and Squirrel and how tricky they both were. I'm embarrassed that I allowed myself to be used like that, but it wasn't my fault because he promised me something and then didn't deliver.

Starring in a fable is a big opportunity and I couldn't resist. And I wasn't exactly surprised when Dragon asked me: I was about to be crowned Acorn of the Year, which back home is quite an honour. Being an extra ruined my career. There would have been dozens of offers for me, but once I appeared in Kelly the Green Dragon (it makes me mad just saying the title!), my career was over.

At the time I believed that we were all going to seek our fortune, Dragon and Squirrel as fablemakers and me as a star. Well, I heard that Dragon and Squirrel never spoke again after that fiasco. But I've done quite well for myself. Every day, hundreds of squirrels line up for a peek at my perfect form. The curator was most kind in placing me pale side down in the display cabinet.

I don't stay in touch with Dragon, but I heard he went back home. Nor with Squirrel. He was jealous of my talent and I didn't return his calls, so I don't know what happened to him.

I just love living in the big city. I couldn't bring myself to go back to that culturally starved community in the forest. My family has come to accept what I do. At first they felt that exposing myself in a museum for a living was indecent, but they don't understand show business.

I auditioned for this job. It's what I wanted. No one made a victim of me; as the country's largest acorn I'm very content to be in this museum. I've been bestowed with a great honour. So I don't want anyone out there feeling sorry for old Acorn. I'm doing just fine, thank you.

First impressions: Acorn is a tongue-in-cheek portrait of someone arguing for his own limitations. He's a victim of his beliefs and right from the beginning he does not follow his heart. Take his example as a chance to listen to your heart when you know something isn't true.

Set your intention for the week: Take a step back and observe where you may have wandered from your true path. Have you bought into something that you know isn't right? This week, allow your heart to support you in taking responsibility. Set your intention to truthfully speak your heart's knowledge. Ask yourself: "Am I waiting for someone else to fulfil a promise I intuitively know they've no intention of keeping – just to prove that promises to me are broken?"

TUESDAY

COLOUR REFLECTION

What does Green Acorn say to you? Green Acorn represents the seed that will one day grow into a mighty oak. The potential here is to understand our deep desire to be loved and to share love. Anything unable to grow in the heart will be revealed through Green Acorn. Therefore the colour of Green Acorn represents that which will grow – or will not grow – from your heart. While we can see clearly the pain of Green Acorn, can we perceive and admit our own deep desires to be loved? Today, pay attention to your heart; is it heavy or full? Become aware of what's true in your heart. When you're wounded by your heart, it's because your heart has been ignored. Listen to it.

WEDNESDAY

JOURNAL JOURNEY

Find your inspiration: If Green Acorn appeals to you, it's time to take a good look at something that you may be in denial about. Remember the adage that there are three sides to any situation? Yours, theirs and the truth. Are you unfairly putting blame for your inability to progress on a person or situation? Look closely at any inaccurate stories that you're telling yourself and others.

Acorn reminds you to come down to earth. It's important that you don't use anything as an excuse to avoid seeing your own role clearly. Look at your past experience as an opportunity to know yourself better, not as something to hide behind. Green Acorn asks that you don't make excuses anymore. And don't forget to see the lighter side of whatever situation you're in.

Today, open up your journal and finish this statement "The truth is _______." Continue to fill out this statement over and over. Don't rush this exercise. It can have remarkable results. Doing this in my groups I've noticed how many people are amazed when their heart speaks the truth to them. Open your heart and allow it to talk to you. Ask your angels for more information. Keep going until you *know* it's over. Trust that process.

THURSDAY

MAKE A CONNECTION

Connecting with yourself and others: In both these exercises you take stock of how you've put other people in the wrong and explore what you really need from those who've disappointed you.

The group exercise in particular, in which you have a chance to hear what you need from a person who's hurt you, can be life-changing.

Solo exercise: Write about what it means to you personally when someone disappoints you. Describe your feelings. You can start by filling in these statements; the final sentence is the most important. What is it that you really need that person to do? Write it out even if they can't do it.

- "Because you disappointed me, I _______."
- "I'm angry you didn't show up for me because _______."
- "What I really need you to do is _______."

Group exercise: We're going to explore the same concept, but here you have your group to work with. Choose someone to play the person who's disappointed you. Now, go through the three statements from the solo exercise. It's vital that your partner only listens as you speak, except when you make the final statement of what you really need your partner to do, when the listener may acknowledge that they'll do that. For example, in one group the person sharing said that all she needed was her father to say she'd done a really good job. When the listener, who was playing her father, said that, this woman felt, in her own words, that her "soul and heart were healed".

FRIDAY

MEDITATION MOMENT

Going within: As we play out the movie of *your* fable, what role have you assigned yourself? Are you the lead? Or just a bit-part player in an old story? Today, choose to open your heart fully and take on the risk of living fearlessly in your heart chakra. If you've done this week's work, you'll begin to see a large shift in your life.

MEDITATION

See yourself sitting in a cinema. As the movie begins, you watch a scene from your life about a dream that never came true. Maybe you'd wanted a promotion, a new house, a relationship – something you were promised that did not come to pass. Allow yourself to feel the disappointment again. Now rewrite the scene. How does your new fable end?

GOSSIP

Charmaine Chartreuse

This Week's Focus: I never met a person I didn't like.

MESSAGE OF THE WEEK

This week the focus is on the power of being true to your own heart. The message of this fable is to live through your heart, no matter what the circumstances. Become aware of when you're seeing others through love – and when you're not. What is the cost of not being true to your heart?

TORI'S TIP

Allowing others to see into our heart requires great courage. Regardless of how others interpret her actions, Charmaine continues to live in a loving state. The legacy Charmaine leaves us is that seeing the beauty in everyone is personally fulfilling – and ultimately a great teacher for others.

MONDAY WEEK 25

THE FABLE OF CHARMAINE CHARTREUSE

Charmaine Chartreuse lived on the edge of town in a mansion with wrought iron gates that squealed when they were opened. The woods had long spread to cover the driveway and any visitors had to venture on foot to the top of the hill.

Charmaine had been left the estate by her parents. She was a friendly woman who knew everyone in town by name. She didn't want to impose on anyone, but she never missed an opportunity to say hello. She looked forward to her daily walks to see the townspeople.

Her first stop was always Plum's fruit stand. She'd often stand across the road and watch the customers come and go for a while before moving on her way. "Wish she'd buy some fruit instead of staring," Plum would mumble to himself.

Charmaine loved the selection of scarves in Ivy's boutique - every day she'd stop in and admire them. On Friday morning, like clockwork, she'd buy one. She asked Ivy lots of questions about scarves, about the material, how to tie them, and so on. It was all very interesting to Charmaine. Ivy would shake her head after Charmaine left. "She's strange. She needs to get a life!"

Charmaine had spiky silver hair and she took great care of her long nails. Every Wednesday she visited Olivia's nail salon. She always tipped Olivia extra, "For that boy you have in college." Olivia appreciated Charmaine's money, but the moment she'd leave, Olivia would turn to the girls. "Do you believe her? That woman wants me to use a whole bottle of polish on her claws every time!"

Every two years Charmaine painted her house Chartreuse green. Mrs Grant from the historical society rolled her eyes. "She has no regard for history or tradition. I mean, it was a beautiful, warm brown for so many years, for heaven's sake!"

At night, inside her mansion, Charmaine would dance and drink her favourite wine as she sang along to Madame Butterfly, always crying at the end. Once a week, Steve delivered her groceries. He usually lingered for a few minutes to talk about art. When his friends asked him about the "weird old drunk", Steve just changed the subject. Miss Chartreuse never made fun of him for wanting to be a painter or mocked his sexual preference.

When Charmaine Chartreuse came to the end of her life, all the townspeople came to the estate auction. Inside the barn, which had been converted into a studio, they stopped short at the sight of Charmaine's paintings. The barn was full of them. "Breathtaking," Plum murmured. The picture of his fruit stand was quite remarkable in its detail.

Olivia recognized the portrait of herself giving a manicure. She put on her glasses to read the title: "My Friend the Manicurist". Olivia glanced at Ivy, who was staring at Charmaine's magnificent paintings of her scarves.

It was Charmaine's series of historical landmarks that caught Mrs Grant's eye, impressing her with their accuracy. Mrs Grant made her decision. Charmaine's home, which she'd left in the care of the historical society, should remain Chartreuse for ever. Brown was, after all, quite common.

And to Steve, Charmaine Chartreuse left all her paints, brushes and blank canvases, for she knew he was a true artist and as unique as she was.

First impressions: When the townspeople realize that their hearts were closed to a woman who loved them deeply, there's great sadness. They learn that Charmaine's legacy of love is very much alive. Can you look into your heart and see the legacy of love that your grandparents left you?

Set your intention for the week: This week open your heart and be loving. Apply this approach even to multi-generational healing. If you view your grandparents through your heart, your vision of them becomes very different. Try to look through your heart at the legacy of love that you've been left by your forebears, even by those you never met.

TUESDAY

COLOUR REFLECTION

What does Chartreuse say to you? Charmaine Chartreuse represents the ideal balanced emotional life - a truly open heart. Chartreuse is a brazen colour and indicates an openness that could push people away. Yet there are many who'd relish this loving openness if they only knew what it was. The loudness of love is softened by its intention. Have you ever noticed that some people's unabashed enjoyment alienates others? We're sometimes frightened by what's foreign to us. Today, ask yourself how familiar you are with the concept of true enjoyment of the heart.

WEDNESDAY

JOURNAL JOURNEY

Find your inspiration: Charmaine Chartreuse asks you to begin finding the good in others. If we don't appreciate those around us, we lose the wonderful gift of who they are. Thinking the best of another person is more powerful than putting them down.

This fable warns that you may be wasting energy. Gossip is an indication that you're not focusing on your own life. What we think of others may not represent the truth of the matter. Beware of speaking ill of another person, for the things you say will come back to you.

"Doing your own thing" may leave you lonely. An aloof attitude can lead others to believe that you don't like them, even if that's not true. If you're feeling cut off, consider that others may be waiting for you to reach out to them. Be kind, even if others are behaving in an inappropriate way.

When we see the best in others, it's because we also see it in ourselves. "If you spot it, you've got it." Today, take a few minutes to write in your journal answers to the following questions:

- What are the qualities you most admire in your friends?
- How would your life shift if you praised others more frequently?
- Are you surrounding yourself with like-minded people who support your growth?

THURSDAY
MAKE A CONNECTION

Connecting with yourself and others: Today's exercises are similar to each other, but the experience of them is quite different. In the solo journey you notice how the words you speak about others uplift your world. In the group activity you see how your words directly impact another person.

Solo exercise: For one week, "gossip forward". Talk behind other people's backs, with one caveat: you must say kind, wonderful and complimentary things about everyone. Remember that you can't compliment them directly. Oh, and don't lie! You must be able to find something sincerely wonderful about the person you choose to speak about. See how your world transforms.

Group exercise: One person sits with their back to the group, which is seated in a tight semicircle. This person remains silent for three minutes, while one at a time the group gossips about that person. Nothing negative, sarcastic or untrue may be said. This is important, as positive statements send empowering energy into the soul of the person under discussion. Each group member takes a turn in the solo seat. After the exercise everyone shares their experience.

FRIDAY
MEDITATION MOMENT

Going within: This meditation helps you to understand projection. Who are you judging and what are you judging them for? Is there a part of you that you're being too hard on as well? Breathe, float above it and see what's going on. Who are you being?

MEDITATION

Visualize someone you may be judging harshly. Notice how powerful your negative feelings are. Picture yourself in a room with that person and tell them what you like about them. If you run out of things to say, start repeating. You can accept this person as they are. Allow them to tell you things they like about you. When they finish, thank them for coming.

PERCEPTION

Emerald Stone

This Week's Focus: The heart knows what the eyes cannot see.

MESSAGE OF THE WEEK

Have you noticed that you can look at the same situation in a different mood and have a completely different take on it? This week we'll play with changing our perception to shift our reality.

TORI'S TIP

When I work with the chakras in my multi-generational healing work, the most profound awareness occurs in the heart chakra, particularly concerning the ways we perceive our ancestors. Remember that we're never fundamentally unhappy; rather, we value our life according to our present perception of it.

MONDAY WEEK 26

THE FABLE OF EMERALD STONE

The young princess hated her life. People waited on her hand and foot and she never did anything unsupervised. One day, in a trance, she wandered far into the garden that surrounded her palace. It had long been untended, the flowers smothered by decaying undergrowth.

Determined to get away from the people who looked after her, she clawed her way through the brambles and came upon a shimmering stone. It was odd to find something so polished, so perfect, in a place this wild. A single ray of sun filtered through the surrounding bushes and made the stone glimmer. It was the Emerald Stone, so beautiful and perfectly formed that she just had to touch it.

When her fingers felt the smooth stone, it spoke. "If you want things to change, you must walk through the sacred door."

She jumped back in alarm. Beyond the stone, barely visible, there was indeed an old wooden door. Hesitantly, she opened the door and peered in to see a hallway, narrow and dark. She took a deep breath and stepped inside. She'd always understood that entering the Corridor of Life would frighten her; that's why she'd never tried before.

She knew darkness, so she was able to breathe deeply and adjust to the small space, until the door slammed shut. She whirled around and grabbed at the door, desperate to run back out into the light, but she couldn't open it.

Finally, calm descended upon her. She understood that she couldn't go back. Her mind raced. What if she got "there" and it was the same old thing she'd always had? What if she was stuck here and couldn't get out? She chose to step forward.

The corridor grew narrower, but she held her head high and the cool air was refreshing. She felt empowered by her daring. The space around her began to expand.

She came to an abrupt halt when she sensed a wall ahead. She reached out and her hand fell upon another handle. She didn't want to leave this place; she'd come to thrive on the energy here. What if there was nothing for her on the other side?

She wanted to race backward; instead she pushed the door open. Light streamed in. Outside, amid flowers, butterflies flew and birds sang. It was familiar and magnificent.

In the middle of this superb garden sat the Emerald Stone. She was looking at the very place that she'd seen only moments before. The Emerald Stone glistened as brightly as before, but now the surrounding garden was equally breathtaking.

"What happened?" she asked the Emerald Stone.

"You entered the Corridor of Life to find your true vision," the stone replied.

The princess laughed – why had she run from here? Everything was wonderful. She was elated.

"This place is a miracle," she murmured.

"Thank you," the stone replied. "I'm happy to welcome you to the place of your new awareness."

She smiled at the wise stone. "I lived out there before, but I live here now." She pointed to her heart. She'd found her home.

First impressions: At first glance we might wonder why a person who has so much feels that she has nothing. What's illustrated here is the idea that we must be willing to go into our own dark night of the soul to change our perception. Often we fear the dark hallway, even though we know in our heart that we'll feel better once we've passed through it.

Set your intention for the week: This week, ask yourself if what you perceive is perhaps not accurate? What if you've been profoundly loved all along? What if, by pushing you away, a parent was trying to avoid passing pain on to you? This week set an intention to go deeper into your heart of understanding. You could make your intention this line from the Prayer of St Francis: "Grant that I may not so much seek ... to be understood as to understand."

TUESDAY
COLOUR REFLECTION

What does Emerald say to you? Emerald sparkles with clear, honest motives. It's the colour that makes one fearless when taking emotional risks. It denotes the pure energy of an open heart and shows love and willingness to others. It lends a steadfast ability to follow through on tasks. The energy of Emerald is one of endurance. Today, consider being willing to break a particular pattern by changing your perception of an issue that relates to your heart. Try to centre into your heart as you contemplate this.

WEDNESDAY
JOURNAL JOURNEY

Find your inspiration: If Emerald Stone sparkles for you, it means that you're now developing a new perception. Emerald Stone welcomes you out of the dark and into your heart. Your reward will be a closer relationship with yourself.

No matter where you are at this time, you can't go back to where you've been. Emerald Stone is inviting you to forge ahead on your path. Forward movement is necessary to change your entire perspective on life - for the better. There are times when no explanation is possible for the things that happen to us. Knowing why is often the booby prize. True peace comes from acceptance of what is and a reinterpretation of the story you've told yourself.

Today, as you prepare to journal, imagine waking up as if you're a neutral observer of your life. Write down the ways in which you perhaps have misjudged yourself. What do you notice?

THURSDAY

MAKE A CONNECTION

Connecting with yourself and others: In these exercises, you explore the effect that changing your perception has on your experience of reality. What's revealed for you? If nothing is revealed, ask Spirit to give you the willingness to change your perception.

Solo exercise: Make a list of all the things that are wrong with your life. Share your list with a close friend. Ask them to hold a neutral space for you, one with no judgment. Now, go back over your list and reread it as if it were a gratitude list. In one sentence, say something wonderful about each item. How has your perception changed?

Group exercise: In this exercise, group members each share a personal change that occurred through altering their perception of a particular situation. What was each person's breakthrough? What was their experience? As you discuss, try to see each situation through the heart, with love.

FRIDAY

MEDITATION MOMENT

Going within: Meditate with Emerald Stone and listen to the feedback you receive. Be aware that anything that comes from Emerald Stone in this meditation is a message from your own heart. Does your heart long for something? Ask yourself what needs to be healed so that your desire can be revealed.

MEDITATION

Begin to imagine the Emerald Stone. When you see it, place it in your "untended garden". Feel waves of Emerald light filling you with courage. Emerald Stone may have some thoughts to help you. Listen carefully. When you are ready, see what has changed in your garden.

GROWTH

Grass

This Week's Focus: Your message is best expressed when you are uniquely you.

MESSAGE OF THE WEEK

One of the most profound lessons that can come from Grass is about having the courage necessary to "be a stand" for who you are. Grass declares that he's gay and owns who he truly is. Every one of us in our life at one time or another must "be a stand" for who we are. The truth of the heart will always come out.

TORI'S TIP

If we take a broad view of the meaning of this fable, we begin to see the tenacity and courage that any person from a minority group needs to stake a claim and take space that's rightfully theirs. Think about what is rightfully yours – and what it would take for you to grow into it.

MONDAY WEEK 27

THE FABLE OF GRASS

Grass was hiding under the snow. He was excited, ready to show himself to the world. He was proud, too, for he was finally confident enough to declare who he was. The winter thaw couldn't come soon enough for the little blade, but come it did. In early spring not everyone was up yet, so there was plenty of room in the field to frolic with those plants that had also awakened early.

One day, well into spring, he told his best friend, Weed, his news. "I'm gay," he blurted out, unable to contain his joy.

Weed looked at him for a moment. "Kidding, right?"

Grass shook himself to indicate a firm "No."

"Hey, listen partner, we'll get you some help. You'll get over it," his friend said reassuringly.

"I don't want to get over it. This is who I am."

Weed said he understood, and pretended to, but it was obvious that he didn't know how to respond. Weed began to avoid Grass. He just watched as Grass was picked on by the other blades, too afraid to stand up to the bullies. He didn't want them to get the idea that he was gay, too.

Grass tried to ignore the name-calling. He often cried when he was alone, but never in front of anyone. Mostly he cried because he missed his best friend.

When he was alone he longed for the day when he could have a boyfriend, like his sister. But Grass was cut down whenever he tried to stand tall. For years he was turned down for work he was well qualified to do. One day he applied for an apartment, but the manager of the building turned him down without explanation. This was the last straw. Grass got mad. His friends told him to forget it, but Grass had to take a stand. He went to a lawyer. "He's doing this because I'm gay!"

Grass took the owners of the apartment building to court and won. Now he could live where he wanted. He threw a party in his new home, but the manager didn't share his enthusiasm and soon the police were knocking at the door. The first week, his apartment was broken into and his things were trashed. His friends begged him to move, but Grass refused. "No one's going to scare me off!"

Two days later, Grass was found in his apartment, badly beaten and close to death. His parents rushed to the hospital. When they arrived, no one could tell them anything. They found the waiting room packed with people who knew Grass, talking about the son they barely knew.

"Who would do this to him?" One blade was in tears. "Grass has always been there for me."

"Grass took me in when no one else would. That boy is an angel."

Another blade stood on a chair. "Excuse me, people. Can we all say a prayer for our friend?"

The room fell silent. The blade began, "Oh, Mother Earth, please make Grass well again. He's a friend to everyone. He took some of us in when we were homeless, fed us when we was hungry ..."

" ... and understood when no one else could," another blade added.

The door opened and a doctor entered. "I'm sorry," he said to the silent, waiting crowd. "There was nothing we could do."

Of all the weeping crowd, one blade felt the full extent of his loss. Weed knew now what he'd lost. He'd lost being there for a friend who'd never stopped loving him.

First impressions: In the fable Grass dies because he chooses to take a stand for what he knows to be right. This lesson is a great gift to those around him. In your response to the fable, take stock of the five people closest to you. Why are they in your life? What lessons do you share? Are you all honouring one another's journey?

Set your intention for the week: Can you look through your heart deep into your own family history and see what it is that your ancestors had to take a stand for in order to survive? Multi-generational healing offers an understanding that evolution is growth. Accepting the choices that others make reveals the depth of love we're willing to allow into our life. This week set an intention to honour the choices made by others, even by your own family.

TUESDAY

COLOUR REFLECTION

What does Grass say to you? There are many shades of Grass Green, just as a heart may exist in different states, from open to fearful, from loving to expectant. The softness of grass reveals a commitment to what your heart is telling you. Listen. As the colour of Grass matures it inspires you to honour your growth, as well as the growth of others. At any given moment, we exist somewhere on the scale between judgment and love. Today, where is your heart?

WEDNESDAY

JOURNAL JOURNEY

Find your inspiration: Grass says that the time is right for you to move on from anything holding you back from full self-expression. Dare to be different. Be unique. Grass has come to tell you that it's time to grow!

Perhaps you're feeling inspired to change your surroundings, whether that involves a short trip, a period of study in a different place or even moving your home - perhaps even abroad! Or it may be time to embark on a new business project, learn a new skill or start working out to get the body you've always dreamed of. Whatever you do, depart from the mundane. Take the chance you've always wanted. And grow.

Grass reminds you that you may also need to become more in touch with your spiritual side. If you've strayed from the fold, the Great Spirits invite you back.

Transition time! This fable is all about growth: growing up, growing out, moving on. You're going to evolve to the next level. The time is now. Today, write down in your journal the things that you'd begin if you knew that you'd be completely supported. What must you undertake? Is there something that you need to own up to in order to grow?

THURSDAY

MAKE A CONNECTION

Connecting with yourself and others: Whether you choose to work alone and do some writing about someone you think highly of, or explore with your group the unique qualities you possess, do these exercises with the intention of growing your personal awareness.

Solo exercise: Take a moment to think of a famous person whom you greatly admire. They can be alive or long gone. In your journal write down exactly what it is that you respect about them. List the qualities that you admire, and when you've finished note down what you feel is the highest value of this person. Where is this on your list of things *you* value? Can you move it up your list? What would your life look like then?

Group exercise: Working around the circle, each person tells you of a quality you possess that they feel is especially yours. Allow each one to say a sentence or two about your uniqueness. Sit quietly and accept their remarks. Were you aware of these qualities of yours? Hold the space of the sacred during this exercise; let your heart be open.

FRIDAY

MEDITATION MEANING

Going within: This meditation will encourage you to see similarities with other people in your life, as well as notice differences. How do you see yourself in relation to others? How do you gauge your personal growth? Over the next few days or weeks, this inquiry may become an important one. Allow yourself to fall asleep, if necessary, during this meditation as that may be an integral part of the experience.

MEDITATION

Find a peaceful place where you can listen to the sounds outside. In your mind's eye, watch the grass sway in the wind. Imagine yourself as one of many blades of grass and sway in their movement. Notice how you are similar to the others. Then see yourself grow out of the blade that you have chosen to be and walk down the road away from the other grasses. Allow images to come to you as you see a road and wander down it. Where do you find yourself? If you wish, write down what you see.

GRIEF

Penelope and Pickle

This Week's Focus: Grief is love without a place to go.

MESSAGE OF THE WEEK

This week we'll explore the idea that the depth of our grief is directly related to the depth of our love. We enter into relationships with our pets knowing that we'll outlive them. What a powerful example of the risk of love. This week think of how others took risks so that you could be here.

TORI'S TIP

Where there's grief there was once great love. This may be a time of preparing your heart for a new love, as well as recalling one that has passed. Allow little Pickle to remind you of the magic of an open heart.

MONDAY

WEEK 28

THE FABLE OF PENELOPE AND PICKLE

Penelope lost her dog, Pickle.

Pickle was not the easiest of pets. Some days he'd refuse his food or take a dislike to the toys in his basket. He'd bark at nothing in particular and annoy Penelope's neighbours. But whenever Penelope was lonely or sad, it was Pickle who knew how to comfort her. He'd make her laugh by grabbing his toy monkey and shaking it wildly, growling at an imaginary enemy.

The years passed and the day that Penelope and Pickle had feared finally arrived – the day when Mother Earth would call Pickle back to her.

Now that Pickle had grown older, Penelope often came home during her lunch hour to visit her ailing pet. The spring sun gleamed through the blinds. She searched the house, but Pickle was in none of his usual spots. Penelope heard a sigh from the bedroom and discovered Pickle hidden among the pillows on her bed. She cuddled him, his eyes met hers and the years they'd spent in friendship were shared in that moment.

He took his final breath, smiled at her and left the Earth. The sun didn't stop shining as she buried her beloved in their yard. She spent many hours mourning her dear friend and the tears flowed in an unending stream of grief. She missed him.

When she told people that her pet had passed away, they were sympathetic for a while. When a few weeks had passed and Penelope was still sad, they suggested that perhaps she needed professional help with her problem.

But Penelope felt that there was nothing wrong with grief – pure grief. Her sense of loss was natural. She'd met Pickle when he was still a puppy, while she was at college. He studied with her, sweated out finals with her and saw her through graduation.

He was there when love hit for the first time and when divorce took nearly all she owned. She'd spent all her twenties with him and he'd spent his entire life with her. They'd been a team. She missed her friend. She mourned the passing of time.

Pickle missed her, too, and for a time hovered near by as she cried over him. As her tears streamed, Penelope knew that loving Pickle had been worth all the pain. In time, when she was ready, she'd love again.

First impressions: In part this is a study of deep aloneness. When Penelope loses Pickle she isn't supported by others and she must allow herself to honour a love that's no longer in physical form.

Set your intention for the week: We all feel unsupported at times. This week, acknowledge the way you process your own emotions. Set one intention to allow yourself to tap deeply into grief when it comes up, and another to support others when they're in a difficult space. Give the support you feel has been denied to you, so that you can experience it yourself.

TUESDAY

COLOUR REFLECTION

What does Pickle say to you? Pickle is the green that heals. Open your heart and surround yourself with green when you wish to extend healing to others or to yourself. Physical illness appears when grief is suppressed. Pickle is about going back to an emotional wound that's still open in order that it may be fully healed. Is there a moment in your past or present that still aches in your heart? Today, consider that ache as grief and honour the love that you feel is no longer there. Allow your heart to mend.

WEDNESDAY

JOURNAL JOURNEY

Find your inspiration: Grief is a part of life. If this fable resonates with you, it's important to remember to accept those close to you and love them as fully as you can while they're present.

This fable asks you to understand your own or another person's grief. Our experiences of loss are as different as we are as individual. Pure grief is the highest emotion, as it mourns loss and nothing else. Grief is love. Well-meaning friends attempted to get Penelope professional help for her grief, but grief is a perfectly normal emotion, not necessarily something needing to be fixed.

Penelope and Pickle knew the value of their relationship. It's sad that they lost one another, yet the strength of their love allows Penelope to find love again. A cycle must be completed to start over. Allow all the mourning to come. If you do, you, like Penelope, will be ready to love again. No matter what, if you choose to walk through this pain, it will be life-changing for you.

Some people run from grief and others deny it. The greatest risk we take is to love someone else and be loved by them. Grief means that we were fully present. Consider the idea that being present for love means risking everything for it.

Is there any pattern you can identify in your life regarding love? Often patterns of the heart are related to a hidden agreement to heal something with our ancestors. Take some time today to journal about any pain or sadness you may have in your heart. As you write, also consider whether this pain is actually yours or someone else's. Sometimes we take on the grief of a relative as a child in an attempt to lessen their pain. Is this true for you?

THURSDAY

MAKE A CONNECTION

Connecting with yourself and others: This part of the journey is about knowing the truth in your heart. In the solo exercise, writing a letter to your grief may offer insight as to why you're experiencing this discomfort. The group exercise is an opportunity to share the ways in which grief can show up in your life. This is a powerful tool for supporting yourself and others when grief comes calling.

Solo exercise: What have you lost? What experience has been painful in your life? Is there a loss that convinced you to stay away from the possibility of love? Take a few minutes to write a letter to whatever you've lost - it could be a person, a place or a thing. Say anything you need to say and clean up this situation. This is your chance to say goodbye and declare the cycle complete. When you're ready, burn the letter and ask to be freed from this imaginary obligation of pain.

Group exercise: In your group discuss the various ways in which grief may have been the real emotion behind any anger or upset. Most importantly, share your awareness of any of the following symptoms of grief (which you may not even have realized were caused by grief): numbness, insomnia, physical pain, lack of faith, regret, trouble concentrating, anger, losing or changing friends, lack of energy, change of appetite, withdrawal. Take time to share disappointment, if any, in friends who you feel let you down. Did you gain any new tools by doing this exercise? Acknowledge each person who contributed.

FRIDAY

MEDITATION MEANING

Going within: In this meditation, you connect in spirit form with someone you miss, recalling the love you once shared together and mourning its loss. By doing so, you create the opportunity to meet with them in that way again. Afterwards, light a green candle in that person's honour. You both deserve it.

MEDITATION

Meditate with Penelope and Pickle, allowing your whole self to emerge. Close your eyes and allow cleansing white light to wash over you. Invite someone you miss into the light. Feel the happiness this moment provides. Tell them how much you miss them and let them tell you the same. Create space for another visit in the future, if you wish.

TRICKERY

Kelly the Green Dragon

This Week's Focus: The tempter is as guilty as the thief.

MESSAGE OF THE WEEK

This fable is a reminder that we manipulate when we're afraid of asking for what we want. This week, we look at how our heart can be open or afraid, and at the ways in which many of our actions are taken to protect us from great disappointment.

TORI'S TIP

Kelly the Green Dragon was the first fable that came to me. In its simplicity it reminds us that when our heart fears rejection, we almost always play the role of the victim or the victimizer. Unnecessary drama is an indication that you may fear losing what you have or not getting what you want – our two greatest fears. Awareness of this dynamic is a powerful tool for creating serenity.

MONDAY WEEK 29

THE FABLE OF KELLY THE GREEN DRAGON

Kelly the Green Dragon's stomach was growling loudly. Outside the cave, snow covered the land. He looked down at the acorn at his feet. It was the Green Acorn, the biggest acorn in the land, but still only a single bite for Kelly. He could almost smell his mother's special acorn porridge. Kelly missed his family and friends back home in the warm south; there, dragons looked out for each other, not like the animals up here. Kelly sighed; perhaps it was time for him to go home.

Down in the valley, Squirrel was hunkering down for the long winter inside his tree home. Adjusting his curtains, he glanced out and saw the biggest acorn ever float by! He ran to the knothole. There was Kelly the Green Dragon, balancing Green Acorn on his tail.

Squirrel just *had* to have that acorn. With an acorn that size he'd easily win the forest's annual acorn contest. He looked over at the pile of acorns he'd collected to get him through the winter. Well, this wasn't about survival ... it was about reputation!

He grabbed a basket and half-filled it with twigs and rocks. Then he scooped up some acorns and strategically placed them on top to make the basket appear to be fully loaded with acorns. Now all he had to do was find Kelly the Green Dragon. He was positive that he could tempt the dragon to swap his one big acorn for what seemed to be a basket of so many. Squirrel delighted in thinking how clever he was.

Kelly was starving now and tired. He needed to stop and take a rest. Green Acorn looked so good to him, but he knew if he ate it now, he'd be even hungrier later. He sat on a log for a moment and began to doze, but his eyes popped wide open when Squirrel, with a full basket of acorns, approached him. He poured on his charm – and so did Squirrel.

"You have a friendly smile," said Squirrel. He set his basket down where Kelly could get a good look at the acorns.

"Thank you kindly," Kelly snorted. He couldn't take his eyes off the acorns.

"That's quite an acorn you have there," Squirrel said, casually rearranging a few acorns.

"Really?" Kelly said as he rolled Green Acorn in front of Squirrel, his stomach growling louder than ever. "Would you like to have it?"

"I really shouldn't ..."

"But of course you can," Kelly reassured him.

As Squirrel reached for the gigantic acorn, Kelly wrapped his tail around Squirrel's basket and lifted it out of view. Squirrel was so overwhelmed, he forgot to offer Kelly the basket or even that he had a basket at all. He thanked Kelly and quickly rolled Green Acorn out of sight.

Kelly could feel the weight of those acorns and his stomach was already thanking him. He waited until Squirrel was well on his way, then dumped out the contents of the basket.

The dragon's roar could be heard throughout the forest. Defeated and hungry, he picked up his few, tiny acorns and continued on his long road south.

Squirrel was disqualified from the acorn contest because he couldn't prove tree of origin. And Green Acorn? To this day he's on display at the Squirrel Museum, but, alas, that's another fable.

First impressions: It's easy to see how each character's intention focuses solely on their own needs. The idea of being dishonest is justified by their desires. As an observer we can see how they're both deceiving one another and how each of them is preying on the vanity of the other.

Set your intention for the week: Have you ever noticed when you feel conned by someone that ultimately you become more angry at yourself than at them, for falling for their trickery? When people sell to our vanity, we often fall prey to our own illusions. This week, set an intention to notice when something truly speaks to your heart versus when it speaks to your ego. Can you see the difference?

TUESDAY
COLOUR REFLECTION

What does Kelly Green say to you? Kelly Green is the colour of unconditional love and an open heart, and represents a deep desire to give and receive love. Kelly inspires us to speak the truth of our heart and asks others to do the same with us. Is there something that you'd like to express truthfully to someone, but fear the pain that you may cause or feel as a result? Today, reflect on the times when you've been truthful and how that brought a great sense of relief, even if it temporarily hurt another person. Allow yourself today to journey into the open heart of Kelly.

WEDNESDAY
JOURNAL JOURNEY

Find your inspiration: When our need for something outweighs our desire to maintain integrity, we're thrown out of balance. If Kelly the Green Dragon stands out for you, there are several factors to consider: first, are you being honest with yourself? Are you really giving everything you have to give in your present situation or are you simply giving up? Are you expecting things to come easily to you? Remember, Kelly was already on his way home when he decided to steal.

Kelly makes us aware of our heart and can reveal where it's empty. This often shows up as a deep-seated fear of failure.

This fable reminds us that we need friends, no matter where we are. It may be time for you to cultivate some new friendships. Help may not come from where you want it to, so you must be open to surprising offers of assistance. Has something that you greatly needed ever come to you from an unexpected source? Today, write in your journal about what happened, including what led up to the event. Write about something that you feel you need – and surrender this need to your angels as you write. Then allow it to be fulfilled.

THURSDAY
MAKE A CONNECTION

Connecting with yourself and others: In the solo journey, you see your true motives and whether or not you've followed your heart. In the group exercise you have a chance to experience the limitations that you yourself place on your heart's desires.

Solo exercise: Consider the motives you may have when you don't ask for what you desire. List a few things you feel you've been cheated out of, such as a job or a relationship that slipped away. Are you 100 per cent honest in being upset or did you know all along that you wouldn't get what you desired? How have you misled yourself? Can you look at your current situation in a new way?

Group exercise: On paper complete the following statement: "If I asked for what I truly desired, it would be _______." Be specific and give details. Don't worry about budget or what you think is possible; write down what your heart really sings for. Now on a separate piece of paper complete this statement: "The reason I don't ask for what I really want is _______." Put both pieces of paper in the hat. Now, keeping it anonymous, pull out a statement and read it aloud. If it's a statement of desire, each person says why it's attainable. If it's a statement of reason, each person states why they understand it. Don't offer solutions or question the reasons. Discuss as a group afterwards.

FRIDAY
MEDITATION MOMENT

Going within: Kelly the Green Dragon is naïve, charming and greedy while Squirrel is a desperate trickster. Which one speaks to you when you meditate on this fable? How does the personality that you identify with offer a message to you?

MEDITATION

Close your eyes, look within ... and see who comes forward to visit you.
Who do you identify with? Greedy Kelly or Squirrel the trickster? Whoever it is,
ask him what he is afraid of. Listen, then ask the Great Spirits for guidance.
Their guidance may come during your meditation or at a later time.
Answers will come when it is necessary for you to have them.

WISDOM

Sage

This Week's Focus: Wisdom is the difference between a calculated risk and stupidity.

MESSAGE OF THE WEEK

In this final week of the heart chakra we learn that we have nothing to prove. The truth of our heart is our wisdom. We know that if we've made it this far and survived, someone somewhere has profoundly loved us. Here we take the final step from our heart to our personal expression.

TORI'S TIP

To be wise is to be in inquiry, a constant curiosity and a holding of space for others to find their own answers. What Sage reveals isn't about imparting wisdom, but about opening spaces. Allowing others to share their wisdom with us is a great honour.

MONDAY

WEEK 30

THE FABLE OF SAGE

"How can I grow old with wisdom?" asked the eager young sagebrush of his grandfather.

"Wisdom comes with making mistakes and learning from them. It's with experience that we learn." The elder sagebrush coughed. He was drying. He knew the time was near for him to transform, perhaps to become a spice or an incense. It was considered a great honour to be chosen as an incense by Mother Earth. To be a sage priest and be chosen for purification is not an everyday occurrence.

"Is that why youth is wasted on the young?" Sage asked.

"Well, there's truth in that statement," said the elder sagebrush. "Those who are young ponder how to keep looking good. Youth concentrates on the things that, as you age, no longer have importance."

He continued, as his young relative listened, "When I was young, I thought the only thing that mattered was being the spiciest of spices. I parted the top of my stalk in a certain way and I'd never roll, only glide. I was busy trying to be spicy. I wanted all the dainty brushes to notice me. No one was more surprised than me when my friend Charlie - just an old branch, if you asked me - was called on to be a sage priest. Charlie became incense! I realized then my foolishness."

Little Sage was puzzled. "Why did he get to be incense?"

The elder paused and looked at the bright young brush. "He was more concerned with the well-being of others than himself. Ah, little one, as I near the end of my existence in this form, I understand that in transformation comes knowledge and wisdom. If I became incense I'd be serving at the highest order."

The young sagebrush was hopeful. "Perhaps someday I'll be incense."

His grandfather cracked his last smile, "True wisdom is in living each day that you have as you are. Don't wish for the day when you become something else, for all you know is now. Live each day to serve and you'll be fulfilled."

It was his time to leave. Young Sage honoured his grandfather's wise words. And today, we still call good advice, "sage advice".

First impressions: Today, simply listen. What would happen if you just listened to someone, instead of trying to give them information? Would their words be betrayed by the truth you hear in their heart? Start now and be still.

Set your intention for the week: Being authentically in the moment gives true wisdom. This week, set an intention to be the observer of when you are present and when you are not.

TUESDAY

COLOUR REFLECTION

Sage is earth green. Our knowing comes from being in true communion with nature. With Sage, the earth energy of brown and green's unconditional love grow together and bring forth the essence of wisdom; this is the true wisdom of understanding that what's important to us can take time to grow. There's no impatience in Sage, for the colour reflects the maturity of your heart. Today, look at the ways in which you've matured and at how your heart is wiser for it. Take into your heart the wisdom of nature and notice your personal cycle. Are you in the bloom of spring? The established foliage of summer? The change of season as the green of your heart fades? Or in the still space of winter waiting for your next cycle to begin?

WEDNESDAY

JOURNAL JOURNEY

Find your inspiration: Sage tells you that it's now time to listen to others. Instead of trying to go it alone, trust that whomever you choose to ask will be the right person to advise you on your journey.

Sage can also indicate the need to surrender what you have no control over. In giving up the struggle, we manifest the wisdom of the shamans. Sage reminds us that wisdom comes only from experience and we all have challenges because we all need the lessons they provide.

Sage offers the opportunity to start over and clean out the old. This could be a perfect time to do it. Rejoice, for if you follow Sage today, you're walking the path of the Great Spirits.

Today, instead of doing and speaking, try to observe and listen through your heart. At the end of the day, write in your journal about what you heard and experienced. Did you listen with a new ear? Did listening through your heart change your impression of what was going on?

THURSDAY

MAKE A CONNECTION

Connecting with yourself and others: Today, be in awe. Notice wisdom coming to you from unexpected sources. See the humanity in everyone and honour Spirit who brought us here. Now try one of these exercises.

Solo exercise: This exercise practises opening your heart to the wisdom of someone else. Ask a friend for their wisdom about something you desire that has eluded you so far. For example, a woman who has a successful relationship is someone who can give you wisdom about love. Make sure you ask her to talk about what she knows to be true about her success. And hush!

If you talk you'll miss her message. Keep an open heart and a closed mouth. Write down what you hear.

Group exercise: In the early fable groups we created an imaginary box of wisdom. It happened quite by accident one night when I jokingly shared that I carry around a box of wisdom. Everyone was eager to know what this box of wisdom was and I laughed. I pretended to reach for a box next to me and placed it on the table in front of us. I then opened the lid, reached in and pulled out a piece of wisdom.

And guided by Spirit, the game began! This became one of our favourite exercises and we often closed our meetings with it. Everyone writes down a question to which they're seeking an answer. People shouldn't share their question, but simply have it with them. As everyone in the group has their own box of wisdom, go around the circle so that all group members can share something from their box with someone of their choosing. Continue until everyone has received wisdom from someone's box. The beauty of this exercise is that no one knows anyone else's questions. You may find it astonishing how intuitive the heart is and how much we know already without realizing. Have fun!

FRIDAY

MEDITATION MOMENT

Going within: During this meditation, be aware of the power of non-verbal communication. As we take a final look at the green chakra, notice how your heart communicates through a gesture, a thought or even laughter. As we move into the fifth chakra of communication, you'll begin to notice how the gestures of your heart are reflected back to you.

MEDITATION

Imagine yourself at a huge campfire. The Great Servant approaches and his energy radiates toward you. He speaks to you not with words, but with energy. Allow the wisdom of the message to reach you. When you have received the message, the Great Servant will depart. When you are ready, come back to your reality. What was his message?

BITTERSWEET

Blue November

This Week's Focus: A window is opened as a door gently closes.

MESSAGE OF THE WEEK

This fable is a poem written by my mother in 1963, one of three that I was directed to turn into fables. There's a longing in this poem that expresses our bittersweet feelings about the transitions of life. This week, be aware that such a longing is a desire to find oneself.

TORI'S TIP

We begin the fifth chakra, the blue chakra, with a personal expression - a poem. All of us have a unique voice to be heard. As you embark on the journey of understanding how you express yourself, you'll begin to see that how you convey the circumstances of your life reveals your participation in it.

MONDAY

WEEK 31

THE FABLE OF BLUE NOVEMBER

We celebrated today.
In the midst of a day filled with grief, we celebrate.
The celebration had been planned;
The birthday child had been told.
How could she know that the telephone and the newspaper
Would this day, a special day to her,
Hold another meaning for those who planned the celebration?
She could not know; we could not know.
The birthday child could not be disappointed.
The news was swift; a good man had passed on.
We wept our tears, we dried our eyes.
We prepared for the celebration.
How to tell a child that our hearts were not gay,
That our thoughts were not joyous?
We could not.
We played our parts: the birthday child was pleased.
The celebration ended. The day ended.
We retired, but the thought that ruled the day stayed on.
The time of the birthday child had passed.
And our friend rightfully claims
The last hour of the day.
So, dear friend, your day has been wrapped with a birthday child.
A celebration.
And, if merriment ruled in our home this day,
So did a sorrow that a birthday child could not see.
A sorrow that you knew was there.
God bless you, departed friend.
God bless you, birthday child.

First impressions: The shooting of America's most vibrant president, John F. Kennedy, in November 1963 was felt around the world. When we learn that this poem was written at that time, we get a new sense of its meaning. It's said that in a sense America lost its innocence that day. In this poem we experience the bittersweet feeling of forging on with happy events even though tragedy rules the day. The fable is about sadness mixed with joy, a feeling that we all understand.

Set your intention for the week: This fable communicates powerfully an emotion that we can all relate to, even if we don't relate to the circumstance surrounding it. This week we begin to look at how clear our own communications are. Are you ready to be heard? Set your intention to observe when you are understood and when you are not. How has not being understood benefited you?

TUESDAY
COLOUR REFLECTION

What does Ink Blue say to you? This is the darkest of blues - nearly black - and it demands to be taken seriously. Its communications are truthful and heavy. There's a sense of profound expression here. Ruled by the fifth chakra, blue is primarily about the ways in which we express ourselves and in Ink Blue we express the deepest part of ourselves. Here the ability to speak personal truths is honoured. Today, keep in mind that others process information in their own way. Remember that the honest truth may be too much for another person to bear. Not everyone can communicate in a deep and meaningful way. This is why people either go or grow. Can you see that?

WEDNESDAY
JOURNAL JOURNEY

Find your inspiration: All things must pass and loss is inevitable, whether that be of a lover, a friend or a job. Blue November reminds you that a release of some kind on your part may be required. Whatever the Great Spirits take away, they replace with something else.

You, like the fable's birthday child, may not even be aware of the loss. But you may feel it nonetheless, for those around you may be grieving - and you'll come to know about their loss. This is a time to remember to be grateful for what you have.

A celebration can often pull you through hard times. Don't be afraid that you're avoiding your feelings by celebrating. In many cultures loss is considered something to celebrate. Your feelings will surface when they're supposed to.

Whatever is coming to you will not be as frightening as it is in your mind. Remember that all passages are a time of grace; if you honour the situation, stand tall in yourself and act for the highest good. Today, journal on how you express yourself during times of loss. Do you try to make everything OK or do you allow yourself to experience the truth of the moment? Without worrying about how good it is, write a poem about your own bittersweet moments. What do you learn?

THURSDAY
MAKE A CONNECTION

Connecting with yourself and others: If a difficult decision is facing you, stand in your truth and wait for the proper time to act. These exercises will support you. The solo exercise will help you to understand a challenging choice made by a parent in your past. The group exercise will reinforce the importance of communicating your love and respect for others at all times, especially when you have to do something that might hurt them.

Solo exercise: Leaders often have to make difficult decisions. Parents, too, make hard choices that may not be understood by their children. Can you recall a time when your parent, or a parent, made a decision that was challenging for them? Were you aware of it at the time? How have you held on to that memory? Have you made a judgment about it?

Write a letter from that person to you, detailing from their point of view why they made that choice. In the letter, make sure they show empathy toward your feelings and apologize for having hurt you if they did. Make sure they sign it with love. Then mail it to yourself.

How does it feel to get this letter?

Group exercise: Take a moment to look into the eyes of every person in your group, to acknowledge and appreciate them. You can do this silently or verbally. When you've finished, write down up to five names of people in your life who you'd love to acknowledge and appreciate. Make the commitment now to your group to contact each of these people within seven days, by email, text or phone. Let your group know what happens.

FRIDAY

MEDITATION MOMENT

Going within: This meditation is about allowing yourself to go into the dark and know that you're safe. Look at the insights you receive through this practice as feedback from the universe. If your life feels challenging at the moment, it reflects a need to change the way you see the world. You may notice how your personal expression is transformed by the work you're doing.

MEDITATION

Imagine stepping into a dark hallway. As you enter, the door behind you shuts. You may feel panic. After a few moments, you hear laughter down the hall - you recognize the voices. A door opens. You have reached your destination. You enter the party and the guests toast you! A friend puts her arm around you. She already knew what you now know, too: the hallway to the light is never an easy place to be.

ISOLATION

Sapphire's Blue

This Week's Focus: I've got all I could ever need, right here.

MESSAGE OF THE WEEK

This week we consider why, if you're ready to participate in whatever you desire, you've not yet taken action. Let's look at the fear-based beliefs that are holding you back from self-expression.

TORI'S TIP

This fable is about how we prevent ourselves from following through on something that matters deeply to us, for fear of failing. In response to Sapphire's Blue, you must determine if you can venture alone on your journey or if you need support to move forward.

MONDAY WEEK 32

THE FABLE OF SAPPHIRE'S BLUE

Sapphire is blue.

He sits in his room all alone. He doesn't like to go out to any social occasion that's beneath him. Why should he? With as many playthings and amusements as he has at home, he doesn't ever have to leave the house. He doesn't have to share his time or his possessions with others. Sapphire wants to socialize, but he's waiting for the perfect invitation.

Last month, he bought a new tuxedo (just in case), but he hasn't needed it yet. He was invited to a baseball game last week, but he didn't have anything suitable to wear. He couldn't borrow anything, as he didn't want the responsibility of looking after the clothes - he might spill something on them. Besides, he had to get up early the next day.

One day Sapphire helped a woman find her lost dog. They met while he was on his daily run - actually he was just finishing or he'd never have stopped to help her. She invited Sapphire to a party, but it was on Saturday night and on Saturday night he loves to read the paper and watch all the shows he tapes in the middle of the night while he's sleeping. Going to a party would have upset his plans. He takes a lot of classes, hoping to make friends, but the people there, well, they're just not of his calibre.

He opens his closet and admires his tuxedo. "Maybe I'll meet someone who'll invite me somewhere I can wear this." Careful, Sapphire, you might spill something on it!

First impressions: In the red chakra, Righteous Raspberry's perfectionism led her to be critical of others, but with Sapphire we see what its like to be truly frozen, forever making excuses for not taking action. What's stopping Sapphire from taking any sort of risk? This fable offers a revealing picture of someone's inability to involve himself in the world. Perhaps Sapphire is suffering from a hidden phobia, a very real fear of what the consequences would be if he left his safe haven. At the end of the fable, we're left only with his dilemma. There's no concrete outcome, no simple resolution.

Set your intention for the week: Is there something that you're truly ready to start doing, but you have yet to embark upon? The blue chakra is about communication and expression and in this fable we see what happens when self-expression is stifled. Remember that all beliefs are fear-based: there's a belief about waiting to engage with the world going on here. This week, set an intention to identify which of the plans that you've been making in your head is ready to become a reality. Start looking at the steps you can take to make this happen.

TUESDAY

COLOUR REFLECTION

What does Sapphire Blue say to you? If your ability to relate to the world is challenged, it can be restored through Sapphire's powerful capacity to heal. Sapphire represents speaking the truth; and when others hear this truth it will resonate with them. It's in Sapphire that we're given the opportunity to overcome whatever is in the way of full self-expression, to transform what has kept us stuck. Today, take some time to consider what you need to heal so that you may step forward and fully express your gifts to the world.

WEDNESDAY

JOURNAL JOURNEY

Find your inspiration: Excuses, excuses. They pile up until you can't see past them. Sapphire wants you to live the life that he can't seem to participate in. If this fable resonates with you, he's saying: "Stop waiting for the right time to live your life!" This isn't a dress rehearsal, it's the real thing. You may be close to achieving a breakthrough on your journey, but if you don't seize the moment you'll lose it. Don't let anything prevent you from taking a chance.

It's important to do the things you love to do, but are you open to new experiences? Or are you stuck in your comfort zone and heading nowhere? Sapphire reminds us that change isn't likely to happen if we carry on doing the same old things. Now is the time to take a risk, talk to people, show up for life! Live now! Don't wait for another day.

If you're treading water or feeling in a rut, it may be because your heart isn't in whatever it is you've chosen. When you feel stifled in the fifth chakra, you may need to look back to the fourth chakra, the chakra of the heart, to determine where the hesitation is coming from.

While the message of Sapphire may be to take action, today is an opportunity to look at whether or not you really want to do so. Take some time to answer these questions in your journal:

- Do I really want to take action?
- Am I hesitating because of fear or an inability to express myself or because I don't really want what I say I want?
- Am I ready to communicate who I am to others?

THURSDAY

MAKE A CONNECTION

Connecting with yourself and others: The solo exercise will establish what you really want right now and how to get there. The group exercise will uncover the challenging beliefs and attitudes that may be shaping your relationships and replace them with empowering ideas for being yourself with other people.

Solo exercise: What do you truly desire? Commit it to paper and look carefully at what you've written. Have you been avoiding something you truly want? Do you keep yourself isolated so as not to fail? When you understand what you've been doing, admit it to someone who's close to you and ask for their loving support in helping you step out of your shell.

Group exercise: Sapphire is very lost. How can anyone help him? He's isolated because he's waiting for the world to come to him. His only solution is to get outside himself. Obsession is keeping him stuck. Go around the circle so that each group member can admit one area in which they're in a rut. Discuss each person's situation and make a firm commitment to support them in moving through their difficulties. Make it your priority to support everyone in your group.

There's a saying that goes: "If you help enough people get what they want, you'll get what you want." How can you, right now, support each person in your group to be free?

FRIDAY

MEDITATION MOMENT

Going within: Is there something that you've been putting off doing? Be aware of the feelings and thoughts that come up through this meditation. Step further back and remember: how you relate to the issue *is* the issue.

MEDITATION

Think of something that you have been putting off - a vacation, calling a friend, painting the house ... Close your eyes and imagine yourself totally involved in the activity. Come back when you're ready. Now, taking action will be that much simpler.

WORKAHOLIC

Brad Blueberry

This Week's Focus: While I worked, my life happened.

MESSAGE OF THE WEEK

More doesn't necessarily mean better. Are you trying to multitask and therefore not giving your full attention and energy to any one thing? For true personal expression through the fifth chakra, stillness and focus are needed. A workaholic rushes to complete tasks at the expense of all else, including good work.

TORI'S TIP

Doing your right work creates true harmony and personal satisfaction. This week may reveal an undeveloped part of your life that needs your focus. You may also uncover a hidden agreement with a family member that needs reassessing. Take a step back from your work; in the long run this will make you more productive.

MONDAY WEEK 33

THE FABLE OF BRAD BLUEBERRY

Brad Blueberry was an artist. He was always working, the busiest and most productive Blueberry in Blueville - and he couldn't understand why he didn't enjoy life.

He hadn't grown up on the "right" vine, like the rest of his friends. He never did feel like he belonged. His friends threw parties and invited him, but Brad would be too busy, working late. Brad knew that when he was famous, he'd fit in just fine.

Brad continued to submit his artwork to galleries, though it was turned down again and again. He'd never give up on any piece. He just put it aside for a while to get some perspective. He spent much of his time alone, waiting for inspiration.

One day, while Brad was up on a hilltop painting, dried-up Old Blueberry rolled over.

"Heh, heh, heh. What you tryin' to do here, boy?" said the old fruit.

"Hey!" said Brad, annoyed by the intrusion. "You're blocking my light."

The older berry leaned in closer to look at Brad's work. "You been up here a long time, think you need a break?"

"I've got to finish this."

"I was once a fresh young blueberry myself. Too busy to be botherin' with fun and parties, though. But then I started to dry up ..." The old berry almost rolled off in a fit of coughing. Brad reached out to support him, but Old Blueberry waved him off. "I learned if it isn't mostly fun, don't waste your juices on it! See boy ..."

He motioned Brad closer, and whispered in his ear. "You're a Blueberry and a Blueberry needs other berries. Nothing great ever happened without some fun sprinkled on it, so *live your life*! Go see something new. Don't get to be a dried snack before you realize that."

Brad glared at the annoying berry, then turned his back on him and carried on painting. But as he bent over to put his palette down, he noticed his wrists. They were looking a bit brown ... and there was a wrinkle! It was starting already. He was drying up!

Brad panicked. He ran after Old Blueberry. "Want to go vine-hopping?" he shouted.

The dried-up old fruit laughed. "You run along now, youngster. You'll finish the picture soon enough."

Brad handed the elder berry his palette. "You finish it, sir."

And with that, Brad was off. Rumour has it that he wound up his life sailing round the Caribbean. One thing's for sure: he never forgot the words of wise Old Blueberry.

First impressions: Brad Blueberry reminds us of the importance of having a special pursuit - but is yours at the expense of other parts of your life? Tunnel vision means overlooking other things. Take time today to take stock of the areas of your life that may require attention.

Set your intention for the week: Notice where in your life you're pushing hard. When we're chasing a deadline, we can shut out everything else and then find ourselves too busy to think about exactly what we're trying to achieve. Brad Blueberry reminds us that we need to know what it is we want to communicate, before we act. This week, set your intention to determine what you'd like to express to the world before you embark on the task.

TUESDAY

COLOUR REFLECTION

What does Blueberry say to you? Brown's down-to-earth quality mixes with purple's higher consciousness to give Blueberry its practical spirituality. Blueberry asks that you use your instincts and follow what you know inside to be true. Blueberry gives us a message that we're guided. It offers us the truth of faith. In Blueberry, you're not afraid to uncover the truth. Let Blueberry work for you. You too must understand, like Brad, that the universe gives you feedback on your actions. Today and all this week, be open to the universe's feedback as you examine your personal expression in life. How is that showing up? Are you balanced? Are you happy? Be in inquiry.

WEDNESDAY

JOURNAL JOURNEY

Find your inspiration: What are you so busy for anyway? Are you using your career as an excuse not to live your life? Sometimes, busyness is a way of masking what's really at stake. Are you afraid of other people? Is there something that needs doing, that you're putting off?

Brad says go live! There's more to life than work. You must set aside whatever is driving you to lose balance, and regain some perspective on your life. You may be shutting others out or closing down parts of life. Get in touch with Brad and consider if you need to change your focus.

When we become as busy as Brad, we've lost sight of our heart. This can show up as saying, "When I'm successful, then I'll enjoy life." It can show up as feeling that you have one last chance at doing something, so you have to hurry! It can show up when someone takes time off work to finish a project and the creative juices are just not flowing and they can't understand why. In Brad Blueberry we learn that all creativity and communication has an energetic flow. There must be a balance of energy in order to create. For artists, creative expression is their life - but even artists have to rest.

Today ask yourself: "What am I here to communicate? What's my gift?" Remembering that nothing lies in the way of your true self-expression, take some time to journal about what you'd like to create and what you'd like to accomplish for yourself.

The fifth chakra reminds us of the legacy we're here to share with others. What is yours? How will you know when you've succeeded?

THURSDAY

MAKE A CONNECTION

Connecting with yourself and others: Both exercises look at what true self-expression is and at how those around us already see exactly what we do to delay our own game.

Solo exercise: This exercise is about exploring the quality of your life as it is currently. It's also about becoming aware of the things that will never have an ending and perhaps creating a conclusion for them. Contemplate these questions: "Am I excessively busy? Am I using anything as an excuse for not going ahead with my personal form of expression? Is there something that I've been 'meaning to do' for ever, but just haven't got around to it?" Now take a few minutes to write about your perfect day. It's OK to mention your dream job, home or relationship, so long as what you say is true to you. Stay away from unrealistic statements that don't feel true. Instead, paint a picture of the life that will serve your best self. What do you notice?

Group exercise: Each group member writes down on separate pieces of paper a few goals that they've not yet reached, and puts them in a hat. Each person now chooses one (take another if you pick your own) and gives a reason why they've been delayed with the goal they chose. The power of this exercise is the opportunity to see how someone else describes your hesitation. Take turns until all the pieces of paper have been drawn.

FRIDAY

MEDITATION MOMENT

Going within: Today you invite a little magic into your life. Release your inner mystic. What visions come forth?

MEDITATION

Imagine completing something you are excited about. Now, stretch your arms out. Become aware that you are floating on water. The water is at the perfect temperature and in harmony with your body. The Lady in the Lake is holding you. Feel yourself twirling freely and playing in this space. She invites you to relax into her. After all, we all wrinkle in water. Enjoy.

VANITY

Aqua People

This Week's Focus: I need more, better, bigger. Yes, that will make me OK.

MESSAGE OF THE WEEK

This fable represents people who work together, but are not truly connected. Even though the terrifying experience of the rising floodwaters forces them to work together, ultimately they do not really relate to one another. This fable is about shallow friends and how the price of vanity may be too high in the long run.

TORI'S TIP

This week you begin to notice that who you are in the world is showing up in the people you surround yourself with. The wise elder of this fable represents your higher self and is here to remind you that how your life occurs directly correlates with the energy your soul puts out.

MONDAY — WEEK 34

THE FABLE OF AQUA PEOPLE

Mike stood on the balcony of his high-rise apartment with his business partners, Crystal and Peter. From inside came loud music and vapid conversation. As the city danced in lights beneath them, Mike toasted the night with his glass. "We've worked for this. We deserve it." They clinked glasses.

"The merger with Mexico will double our value," Crystal said.

"We're going to make more - a fortune!" Something made Peter stop and he turned to face the room. From among the gyrating bodies of the disco, an old man emerged. He looked like Moses, with his robe and staff. The three on the balcony gasped, yet no one inside seemed to notice him.

The stranger nodded to the three. Then, in a low voice that drew them toward him, he spoke. "Very few can see me, for most are too absorbed in their own selves. They seek simply to have."

"Sounds like us." Mike joked.

The man picked up a soda from a table and sipped it. "Strange concoction. But pleasurable. Where I come from, we seek not to please ourselves, but to serve others."

"Where's that?" Peter asked.

"What do you mean, very few can see you?" Crystal interrupted. "Why can *we* see you?"

"Is this a joke?" Peter asked Mike, who'd remained calm. "A party game, right?"

Mike shook his head.

"Do you wish gluttony or generosity?" asked the visitor.

"What kind of a question is that?" said Peter, in his best rational voice.

"Oh, hush," said Crystal. "Please tell us. We want to know the secret."

The stranger replied: "You must no longer ask for more, but do well with what you have."

"OK ..." said Peter, sounding unconvinced.

In an instant they were all standing knee-deep in water, with nothing visible in all directions but clear blue sea. The water was rising. Panic set in.

"What's going on?" shouted Peter. "Where are we? Where's the party?"

"Wait," said Mike. "We're getting *more*!"

"I don't get it," Peter shouted.

"Mike's right," said Crystal. "We wanted more, so we're getting more ... more water!"

"Help!" yelled Peter.

Now rain was falling in torrents and the water rose faster.

Crystal shouted above the rain. "We mustn't ask for more, but do well with what we have."

Mike sang out, "Have fun. Laugh! Enjoy."

As Crystal and Mike began to play, the rain began to let up. Peter joined in, laughing nervously. Finally, the rain stopped. Soon all three were splashing about and the waters began to recede.

They found themselves back at the party. They hadn't been missed. They were standing exactly as they had been, their clothes dry. The old man was gone.

Peter was furious about the trick he thought Mike had played on them. The other two watched as he stormed away, a piece of seaweed caught in his collar.

First impressions: What if you and the people close to you had to work together to save all your lives? If the people you associate with either at work or at home are not vital to you, maybe you need to find new friends - or simply the real you.

Set your intention for the week: This week, notice the people you're inviting into your life. Is there someone who perhaps lets you hide a false place that isn't really you anymore? Set your attention to attract people who mirror your highest personal expression and allow you to be the best you can be.

TUESDAY

COLOUR REFLECTION

What does Aqua say to you? Aqua mixes the communication of blue with the unconditional love of green, and in essence is about speaking to others from the heart. It's the colour of an artist who's connected with a muse and can translate the muse's inspiration to others. Aqua says, "I must tell you how I truly feel." Aqua points out the most important part of your life. What would your world look like if every person in it were vital? Would that change your desires? Would your goals need to be rewritten? Would you "need" goals? Today, think about how you inspire others and offer appreciation to those who inspire you.

WEDNESDAY

JOURNAL JOURNEY

Find your inspiration: This fable depicts getting caught up in our drive to have more. Before you can stop this behaviour, you have to pause and find purpose in what you do have, instead of just having it. If you're not fully using all that you've received, it may be time to give some of it back.

You do have all you need. In fact, if you can't find what you seek inside yourself, you won't find any peace. Nourish what has nourished you.

Today, begin your journal time by noticing what the world is communicating to you. How do you see your own life experiences? Is your life easy or hard? Are you lucky or unlucky? Do you feel blessed or put upon? In the fifth chakra we begin to see that what is showing up in your world is mirroring the energy that you are sending out. Take some time to write about what is showing up in your external life and what may be going on internally to create it.

THURSDAY

MAKE A CONNECTION

Connecting with yourself and others: If you're working on your own, try the solo exercise, which is a mix of visualization and journalling - and also a lot of fun! And you'll be surprised how inspiring this week's group exercise can be, in which you imagine a photo album containing snapshots of your future life.

Solo exercise: Take a moment to go inside, bring down white light from the heavens and allow your angels to come forward into the light with you. Each angel brings a gift and hands you a photograph. Look at the image and get an impression of what it shows, then take a moment to write in your journal what its gift is. Repeat for each of the gifts that your angels bring forward. What did you notice?

Group exercise: Before you on the table is an imaginary photo album. In this album are snapshots of the things that you're going to be doing, having and participating in over the coming year. Open the book and, as you flip through the pages, take time to explain to your group what each picture is and what you're doing in it. Don't forget to tell everyone the importance of these things to you. Allow others to ask questions about your activities. Take turns. As each person speaks, someone else takes notes for that person to review later. What is revealed?

FRIDAY

MEDITATION MEANING

Going within: Sharing gratitude is the intention of today's meditation. As you send out Aqua light to the world, be aware of authentically communicating your love and appreciation for those you know and are about to know.

MEDITATION

Visualize an Aqua light within you. Imagine people you love surrounding you. Feel the light building and spilling onto your loved ones. Send gratitude to those you love and those you have yet to meet. Bless them all. Notice the energy and any messages that you receive. What message are you communicating?

EXPANSION

Sky God

This Week's Focus: "You'll see it when you believe it" – Dr Wayne Dyer

MESSAGE OF THE WEEK

This week we look at who we choose to communicate with. We must remember that the people we connect with perceive us through the filter of their personal awareness. If you're not getting the outcome you desire, you may have to acknowledge that the message you're sending isn't the message being received.

TORI'S TIP

At this point in your journey, become aware of who's presently showing up in your life. Notice that Sky God himself has some powerful peers. Take some time this week to observe the people who are now becoming your wise councillors. They're here to remind you of your best self. Perhaps your world is being uplifted.

MONDAY

WEEK 35

THE FABLE OF SKY GOD

Sky God requested the counsel of Mother Earth and Goddess, two other highly respected Great Spirits. He'd been assigned the job of colouring the heavens. It was a daunting task and he wished to seek the advice of his peers.

"Red would be a wonderful colour for the sky," offered Mother Earth, but Sky God had already chosen red as the colour of warning.

"Yellow is the colour of the sun," Goddess said, "so that won't do ..."

"Green is the colour of my foliage ..." Mother Earth said.

"Orange?" he asked.

For a long moment, they all thought about orange. A bold colour, one of movement.

"Let me ask you this," Goddess began. "What type of feeling do you want Earth dwellers to have when they look up at your sky?"

"I'd like them to feel calm and serene, but I don't believe that's possible."

Mother Earth took exception to this. "What are you saying? Earth dwellers gain tremendous serenity from nature. They love to be around it, and they're all the better for it."

Sky God nodded and Goddess smiled upon him. "You'll only see the colour when you believe what you want can be achieved."

Sky God sat and thought. He stood and thought. He waited and thought. He looked to his wise colleagues. They were watching him.

"What colour are you seeing?" Mother Earth asked.

"I'm seeing a colour. It's light and cool," he offered.

"Do you believe it will do what you want?" Goddess asked.

"I must, because I'm seeing it." Sky God said.

"What shall we call your sky colour?" Mother Earth asked.

"It's blue. It's my blue."

"Then," said Goddess, "we shall call your blue Sky Blue, for it's the colour of your sky."

And so it was.

First impressions: Sky God is the only one of the Great Spirits who has his own fable. He's invited the other Great Spirits into the story as supporting characters. If you're in inquiry in your own life, you can have support if you ask for it. In this fable, even a Great Spirit seeks wise counsel.

Set your intention for the week: Requesting advice isn't an indication of weakness, but rather a sign of strength. This week, set your intention to observe yourself – notice if and how you ask for support and assistance. Does what comes back to you align with what you think you're requesting? It's important that we truly understand the idea that it's the message we're sending that brings us what we get.

TUESDAY
COLOUR REFLECTION

What does Sky Blue say to you? Soothing Sky Blue brings tranquillity and cools our emotions, conveying a message of peace. Sky Blue calms the soul and offers a sense that all is right in the world. The energy here is one of a very expressive communicator. Sky Blue helps you to have an authentic effect on others. Today, imagine yourself surrounded by Sky Blue and allow this colour to guide you in all your communications. Notice how your voice, your energy and your very intention in conversation may shift to create a totally relaxed connection.

WEDNESDAY
JOURNAL JOURNEY

Find your inspiration: When the obstacles to advancing on your journey seem overwhelming, you, like Sky God, need to seek wise counsel. Choose your advisers carefully though; someone who is too critical could destroy your confidence. Often we teeter on the brink of making the right choice and simply give up, for fear of being embarrassed. Don't use another person's negativity as an excuse to hold yourself back. If you pick advisers whom you know will not support you, don't blame them.

When you believe that something is possible, everything and everyone you need to manifest your desires will materialize. We can only create what we can envision. If you're drawn to this fable, then it's time for you to imagine what you wish to create, for you'll only see it when you believe it!

It may be necessary now or in the future to seek wise counsel before you can move up to the next level in your life. To summon this advice, write a letter in your journal to and from your angels. The letter can be as simple as this:

Dear Angels,
I'm writing today to seek your guidance about _______

Complete the sentence, describing clearly what it is you're seeking your angels' guidance about. You could even ask them to send support your way in human form, if you need it. Leave some space on the page, then allow your angels to respond, perhaps like this:

Angels: Thank you for inviting us. We advise _______

Allow your angels to fill in the blank.

THURSDAY

MAKE A CONNECTION

Connecting with yourself and others: Both these exercises are forms of spiritual brainstorming. Whenever you ask the universe for feedback, be open and listen. Ask Spirit for a solution while you sleep and be open to what's presented. When you wake up, write down what you've learned.

Solo exercise: Can you think of a few things that at one time existed only in your mind before they manifested? Make a list. Now make a list of some things that are presently only in your mind's eye. If you've created something before, you can do it again. Share your list with a trusted friend and ask them over the next week to phone or email you as if what you desire is already in your life. This practice can be very powerful. Remember, we all paint our own sky!

Group exercise: Come up with a list of reasons for why something you want is eluding you. Now pick someone in the group to play you. That person sits in your chair and reads your excuses one at a time. Before attempting to confront your own self, have the group offer solutions to the frustrated "you". Watch yourself carefully. Feel free to offer suggestions to yourself. Ask the person who played you how they felt in that role. What have you learned?

FRIDAY

MEDITATION MEANING

Going within: Do you have beliefs that have kept you from fully emerging with your true voice? How have these supported you? Do you have an inner knowing that what you desire is possible? This meditation is about allowing yourself to step into what you know to be true. This is the power of the fifth chakra.

MEDITATION

Imagine yourself in a warm bath. Lie back and visualize soothing, calming water around you. As you lean back, see the sky above you, a breathtaking blue that appears endless. Now, imagine something that you believed to be impossible for you to achieve - maybe your dream job, more money, a divine relationship ... Repeat aloud, "I know this is possible." Say this phrase until you believe it. When you are ready, let it go. If you know your desire can be, it already is.

IMPATIENCE

Electric Blue Moon

This Week's Focus: If I don't take care of it, it'll never happen.

MESSAGE OF THE WEEK

This week reveals the necessity of waiting for the outcome. When we ask our guides to assist us, we must hold the tension to stay focused, even though what we desire may not be in physical form in our life just yet. Don't give up or try to force a situation, but know that what you focus on, you will draw to you.

TORI'S TIP

It's important to notice where you are on your path. For impatience is based on fear and is therefore a block to actually creating something. The key is to allow Spirit and others to assist you in breaking through to the next level in your life. When you reach a plateau, you sometimes must simply wait for the next steps to appear.

MONDAY

WEEK 36

THE FABLE OF ELECTRIC BLUE MOON

Once upon a time there was a boy named Etan who lived beneath a dark sky. The Sky God told him only to believe and light would come, but Etan didn't want to wait.

Determined to make light come, Etan went out and found a used moon. (He was too impatient to make his own.) Now, not only are used moons hard to come by, but their owner is the only source of their energy. Etan didn't quite know what that meant. He was just focusing on wooing the moon away from another person's sky.

"Well," Etan sighed as he hung the moon up in his sky, "at least I'll have some light over here." But he hadn't yet realized what he was in for. The moon wouldn't light up. All that work and still no light! Etan was pretty mad, and he was about to take the moon back to the person he'd charmed it from, when he saw the dangling cord. There it was. A plug! His moon had a plug.

He groped around for a place to plug in his moon, but couldn't find one. Then he touched the cord, by accident, and the moon lit up! It was a spectacular vibrant Electric Blue. The moon lit up the entire sky. At last Etan had his very own light, after being in darkness for such a long time. He stood there holding the cord, admiring his accomplishment.

A moment like this needed proper celebration. Only a bottle of the best sparkling cider would do. But, as he turned to reach for his libation, his moon went out.

He searched in the darkness for the cord and the instant he touched it, the moon was bright and full again. He sat down with a thud, feeling helpless. He said to himself, "The only way for me to have something beautiful is if I never leave it."

That night Sky God sent him a message on the eastern breeze. "The dawn will come when you let go." But Etan didn't want to let go. It was better to cling on to the cord than to have nothing. But all humans must sleep. Growing weary, Etan slumped down and released the cord.

When he awoke, there was a radiant light in the sky, blocked only by the dark outline of his moon. Etan was amazed. He understood now that he couldn't have light all the time.

This was better; for one thing, he didn't have to make it happen. Off in the distance, the Sky God smiled.

First impressions: Remember Sky God from last week's fable? He represents asking for and listening to guidance. Etan doesn't want to listen, so he ignores intuitive guidance and makes a decision based on fear. Are *you* listening?

Set your intention for the week: As you read Etan's story, notice your reaction to his behaviour. If you find yourself in judgment, or if this fable upsets you, it may be that you're closing in on your desired outcome and fear it actually happening! Remember that it's darkest just before the storm and therefore you may be closer than you think to success. This week ask yourself each day: "Am I willing to trust the Great Spirits? What will it take to trust that I am divinely guided?"

TUESDAY
COLOUR REFLECTION

What does Electric Blue say to you? This most dramatic of blues indicates an ability to manifest your spiritual essence and express and create your desires – with big results. Electric Blue makes an impact. When you doubt the manifesting powers of Electric Blue, you sell yourself short and create something less than you truly desire. Today, consider all the ways in which you express yourself and remember what you've already created in your life. Remind yourself: if you've done it before, you can do it again. What you choose to create is well within your ability at this time.

WEDNESDAY
JOURNAL JOURNEY

Find your inspiration: Electric Blue Moon is a reminder not to force an issue. If something feels urgent to you, then maybe your timing isn't right. If you're impatient and make a decision or act before it's time to do so, you may block the situation from working out naturally.

Are you in a relationship that you feel isn't giving you what you need? Stop and make some space for yourself. Even if you think you've given a project or a relationship plenty of time, Electric Blue Moon reminds you to give it more. Think about what you really need and ask Spirit to help, then wait for the outcome. You must give the seeds you've sown the time to come to fruition. You've told Spirit what you need; now be patient. If you try to force something, you may bind yourself to something that you'll come to regard as a hindrance. Allow right action to happen in its own time.

Just stop for a few moments. Now jot down in your journal your thoughts about any situation in your life that you feel is out of control. List three things you can do to find your centre again and step away from the situation. Remember that you may not be ready to resolve it fully. Trying to force something may push it away permanently when you'd have worked out the problem with more time. Answer these questions:

- What's the best way for me to live from my centre again?
- If I knew why I was impatient, what advice would I give myself?
- What do I fear losing when I create my truest desire?

THURSDAY
MAKE A CONNECTION

Connecting with yourself and others: Today, let's look at your beliefs around what you wish to create in your life. If you don't have something that you want, chances are you've been holding on too tightly and driven it away. Here are two exercises that offer you ways of working on this issue, either alone or in a group.

Solo exercise: What is it you want? Where has your main focus been? Write down all you've done lately toward your goals and why you're growing impatient (if you are). Be careful not to shift away from your main focus. Don't give up. Then take a moment to write out an answer to this question: If you knew what was coming to you, what would it be?

Group exercise: If you're pushing things to happen and they're not manifesting, a belief may be blocking your path. For example, Etan believed: "The only way for me to have something beautiful is if I never leave it." So, let's do some belief clearing. First, discuss as a group the concept of "working hard" versus "working smart".

Then take a few moments to write down your beliefs surrounding one particular issue in your life. It's helpful to begin with a lead sentence to answer, such as: "My beliefs about money are _______." ("It's easy to create" or "It doesn't grow on trees", for example.)

You can substitute the word "money" for "work", "love" or whatever belief you sense may be in your way of manifesting a particular experience. Share the lists among the group. When you stumble upon some disempowering beliefs, ask for assistance in creating some empowering ones. Adopt any of the ideas that resonate with you.

FRIDAY

MEDITATION MEANING

Going within: Once you've tried this meditation, spend some time writing down the steps you've taken in the past to successfully complete something. Then consider where you are you right now with your current projects.

MEDITATION

Imagine something you strongly desire. Electric Blue Moon appears and begins to cool the heat of your emotions. You are starting to feel detached from the object of your desire. Allow yourself to be the observer and walk past whatever it is you desire, to continue on your path. Write down any communication you receive in the moonlight – it's a message from the Council of the Great Spirits.

QUEST

Navy Trail

This Week's Focus: When I am somewhere else, my life will have meaning.

MESSAGE OF THE WEEK

The final blue fable represents one of the most powerful aspects of the fifth chakra's energy: unspoken communication. We learn that it's never too late to learn or grow, and that the way we communicate is in fact the journey we're on. This week, take on a state of curiosity and allow yourself to be inquisitive.

TORI'S TIP

Be aware that you may be further along on your journey then you think. When we stand in our truth, what once appeared to be an obstacle is revealed to be simply a belief that's dissolved by our inner knowing of who we are. Notice that your old fear-based belief system is being replaced by a wise knowing of your truth.

MONDAY

WEEK 37

THE FABLE OF NAVY TRAIL

Once upon a time, in the town of Blue, a Navy Trail appeared. It began at the edge of town. All who saw the trail thought it peculiar that it appeared to lead to the swamp. No one was brave enough to follow the trail, for the leeches and bloodsucking insects, not to mention the crocodiles, made it too dangerous.

One day Mrs Patriot, the oldest woman in Blue, decided to leave her home and venture upon the Navy Trail. She went to the wise child of the village to inform him of her plans.

The wise youngster saw her determination. "Are you aware of the darkness on the Navy Trail?"

The woman nodded, "I've learned that the truth is not always the most pleasant option, nor the easiest road to travel, but it's the most rewarding choice. I will cross the swamp."

"Why now?" the child asked.

"I had to be ready." She glanced out the window to the place where she knew the swamp to be. It was gone! Where was it? The youngster giggled.

She turned to him. "How did you do that?"

He shook his head. "I did nothing. The swamp exists to prevent us from facing who we are and what we truly desire."

She looked beneath her feet. The Navy Trail ended where she stood. "It's here under me. Look."

"Yes," he said. "Once you realize that your life is where you stand, the Navy Trail changes."

"What of the others?" she asked. "Will they see the swamp?"

"Anyone who believes that life is better elsewhere always sees a swamp to stop them. Those who realize life is where they are, see the Navy Trail beneath them."

He yawned and stretched. It was time for his nap. He stood to leave. "Remember the Navy Trail cannot tell you what your experiences will be. The Navy Trail always runs parallel to our own. If we choose it, we combine the two paths."

When he'd gone, the old woman recognized that her quest was complete – she'd done what she'd set out to do. She was on her path. As she walked home, the path was laid out before her. Her life had meaning just where she was.

Remember, it doesn't matter where you are, as long as you're there.

First impressions: This fable challenges our presuppositions about wisdom and age. By seeking out a wise child, Mrs Patriot offers us an opportunity to shift our thinking. Who is this wise child? Why is he in the fable? Could he be the symbolic inner child of us all, one who could guide us and send out the energetic message that will attract what we say we'd like to create?

Set your intention for the week: This week be prepared for what you desire to show up in a form that's not what you expect. Set your intention to be open to seeing that your message has been received and an answer delivered in a way that might challenge your perceptions.

TUESDAY

COLOUR REFLECTION

What does Navy Blue say to you? In its most simplistic definition, Navy Blue is true blue. It represents the truth and combines the fifth chakra's message of communication with the unknown, allowing us to uncover the truth. Navy Blue vibrates sincerity, and at the same time energetically offers you an ability to see your own gifts. There's a sense of honour and courage inherent in Navy Blue. In this colour, the desire to take a stand for something you believe in is more powerful than any obstacle. Today, take a moment to think about what you're willing to take a stand for. What is the truth in your life? Allow yourself to be filled with courage and determination, and you'll then know the energy and passion of Navy Blue.

WEDNESDAY

JOURNAL JOURNEY

Find your inspiration: Now's the time to let go of the idea that you're not doing enough. This fable is a reminder that you're already on track and in your own integrity. There's nothing outside you to get; it's already inside you.

We must face who we are and allow ourselves to become what we're meant to be. How often do we hide from something, fearing the pain that comes with awareness? Only by exploring your own truth can you discover if your quest is a valid one.

It's time for you to look at all that you have in your life already. Perhaps you'd do well to ask others how they perceive you. You may be surprised to hear how successful you appear to the outside world. Navy Trail represents the difference between being teachable and unteachable. Don't miss this message of this fable.

You've been "there" all along. The journey is the destination. Become aware of patterns of being busy for busy's sake, which lead you to believe you're not making progress. Enjoy the stillness of the spiritual quest.

In your journal today, take some time to acknowledge yourself for the hard work you've undertaken to get where you are now. Breathe, then complete the following statements:

- In this last year I have accomplished _______.
- I'd really like to get some acknowledgment for _______.

When you're ready, ask a friend to acknowledge you for one thing you feel that you've not been acknowledged for. Journal more on how that experience was for you.

THURSDAY

MAKE A CONNECTION

Connecting with yourself and others: Both these exercises help you to look at yourself and your life with a fresh pair of eyes. Remain open to challenging viewpoints and be brave enough to make a change if you realize that your journey isn't heading in the right direction.

Solo exercise: Phone three people you trust for their honest feedback about your journey. Ask them how they perceive your life. Are you on an unnecessary quest? Or making bold strides? Take notes. Don't get defensive or argue. Stay open to what your universe offers.

Group exercise: This is the 30-second sweep. Imagine that you're in the "supermarket of life" and the shelves are filled with items, some tangible, some not. You have 30 seconds to run through the aisles and load up your cart. Someone in the group times you, while someone else writes down all the things in your cart as you throw them in! When your time is up, present to the group what you've chosen and why. Are there any surprises? Ask yourself, what type of person would have chosen these things?

FRIDAY

MEDITATION MOMENT

Going within: Today's meditation allows you to experience your truths with all your senses. What does it reveal? If you don't have any revelations immediately, be aware of what may surface over the next few days.

MEDITATION

Write down five truths about yourself. Look at your list and close your eyes. Imagine the Navy Trail stretched out before you. See yourself walking along it - go ahead, walk farther than you think you should. On the way, you may see images or hear a song or feel the sun on the path. Allow all sensations. When you are ready, open your eyes. Did you come to any new awareness about your truths?

DESPONDENCE

Violet Iris

This Week's Focus: By taking action, I found the road out.

MESSAGE OF THE WEEK

At first glance this fable may seem to be about taking action, but at a deeper level it indicates that it's only through taking the action that we can see the problem. Violet only opens the discussion about acting to move through despondency. This fable also looks at how a sense of personal emptiness is often passed down in families.

TORI'S TIP

You'll notice that every purple fable is driven by an underlying emotion. As we journey through this chakra, become aware how deep-seated emotions are often inherited. If any of the fables in this chakra resonate deeply with you, check for an underlying quality or characteristic belonging to one of your grandparents.

MONDAY WEEK 38

THE FABLE OF VIOLET IRIS

Iris lay in bed in her farmhouse, wishing that the awful feelings of hopelessness would go away. "I don't want to be here!" she said to no one. She couldn't see the point of living. She couldn't eat or sleep and her agitation worsened as she got hungrier and more tired. No one came to see her. She was lonely, but too depressed to call anyone. Besides, she thought, who would want to speak to her?

Finally, in desperation, she prayed to the Council of the Great Spirits.

Mother Earth appeared. "What do you wish my child?"

"I want to feel better," she said weakly. "Where did this feeling come from? Can you make it go away?"

"If I did that, you'd never know how to get out of the trap you set for yourself. Are you willing to learn how to do it yourself?"

"Yes, Mother Earth."

"Then get out of bed and take a shower. Get ready for your life. Make yourself a good, nourishing meal."

"What?" said Iris, annoyed. "How is *that* going to help?"

"You prayed for a solution. I have one. Are you willing to take it?"

"But it just seems so ... well ...."

"Easy? It is. All you need to do is find your road again." With that, Mother Earth disappeared.

Iris got out of bed and reluctantly did as she'd been told. She took a bath, chose her favourite outfit and did up her hair. She prepared a delicious meal and said grace over the food. She felt stronger once she'd eaten, but still miserable. She prayed once more to the Great Spirits.

"This isn't helping me," Iris whined when Mother Earth appeared. "I still feel horrible."

"That's because you're focused only on how you feel."

Iris didn't understand. "Please, what else is there?"

"Life." And with that, Mother Earth created a hurricane and disappeared.

Iris jumped into action. She got the horses to safe ground and at once remembered the neighbour's children, alone in their home while their mother was at work. She rushed through the storm to get the children out before their house was blown to pieces.

When the winds subsided, Florence realized that life no longer felt pointless. The solution had been there all along: helping others. Soon she began volunteering at the local hospital and eventually found a job there. Through helping others, Florence found herself.

Watching from above, Mother Earth smiled. Why did humans rarely realize how easy solutions could be?

First impressions: Reading the fable, we may conclude that we can get rid of sadness by taking action. And it's true, that works. Yet as we look deeper it's what's missing from the fable that becomes its true essence. Violet Iris sets the tone for the purple fables by posing the question, "Where did this feeling come from?"

Set your intention for the week: How often do we create a temporary fix for a big issue? We're used to putting a bandage on a broken leg and expecting to run a marathon. This week, set an intention to look at the origin of things as they come up. Stay away from asking why something is there; instead, be in inquiry about where it came from. Knowing *why* is the booby prize, knowing *where* is empowerment.

TUESDAY
COLOUR REFLECTION

What does Violet say to you? Violet is intuition. If you've felt compelled to complete something, your intuition is operating in Violet. Faith is strong when you have Violet around you. There's a deep strength in Violet, one that's not often seen in the simple flower. True nurturing and a questioning nature are presented in Violet. In the fable, Iris is despondent. Today, think back to a time when you were overwhelmed by negative feelings and remember how you found a way through them.

WEDNESDAY
JOURNAL JOURNEY

Find your inspiration: If Violet resonates with you, now is the time to take action. However, it may not be the type of action you think. While it's true that the way out of stagnation is to be in motion, action can also involve making a conscious effort to observe and understand your own patterns.

If things seem bleak, your perception is directly related to the meaning you're making of a feeling. There are times when we're too emotionally distraught to know what we really want. If you feel hysterical, remember that the feeling is probably historical. Somewhere in your past you also found ways to cope with challenges - remember these.

One of the most powerful ways to look at the truth of a difficult situation and move through it is to journal. Today, think of the pen you hold in your hand as a sword to cut through tangled beliefs and old ideas. As you put pen to paper, summon your angels and ask them to bring you the profound clarity that you deeply need to cut through old family patterns. Write down what your angels tell you. When you're finished, put away your journal for 24 hours before returning to it and reading what you wrote down. What do you notice?

THURSDAY

MAKE A CONNECTION

Connecting with yourself and others: When you take an action only to find yourself stopped, a hidden family agreement is often to blame. Despondency can then be seen as a surrender to the agreement. In these exercises, we explore different contexts to work with the idea of hidden agreements and how to get past them.

Solo exercise: If a belief is fear-based while a knowing is faith-based, let's look at the beliefs you've created. Is there something you've been close to creating in the past, but something stops you every time you get close? Today, imagine you're standing in a line to claim your dream. You get to the window and a man asks: "What would you like?". Write down your order and imagine waiting for it, knowing it's just about to arrive. Describe your internal experience. How does it feel to walk out the door holding your dream?

Group exercise: In this exercise, everyone in the group shares their beliefs around work, while someone makes notes. Now, knowing that all beliefs are fear-based, take time to discuss the underlying fear of each belief. What would it take to transform each belief into a knowing - something that you *know* in your heart to be true? As a group, become aware of the concept that what you know to be true is empowering, while beliefs are a temporary fix.

FRIDAY

MEDITATION MOMENT

Going within: In this meditation you seek out despondency and the Great Spirits show you the way through it. All that you've done this week has prepared you for this spiritual drill. This exercise will help when you experience a sadness, perhaps of a family member, that may not belong to you.

MEDITATION

Imagine a wide, expansive countryside. The wind blows and without warning carries you to a place of sadness. Notice the odd comfort in this melancholy and grow through it. Look closely at the land and see its beauty. Ask the Great Spirits to reveal the action you must take. You will either intuitively know what to do or it will soon be revealed to you. Open your eyes and see that all is calm. Be grateful.

MYSTICISM

A Woman Named Aubergine

This Week's Focus: You are not to know.

MESSAGE OF THE WEEK

How safe are you in the unknown? Aubergine dares us to trust our inner knowing. The idea of mysticism implies that you already know everything you need to know. The challenge is to accept that you have the tools and knowledge. Mysticism also implies ecstatic faith and the promise that you'll know true mastery.

TORI'S TIP

In ways that may not be readily understandable, Aubergine represents the part of you that must transcend unresolved pain from your family of origin. When you go deep within, you'll find that all you need to know is already in your history. Your purpose and legacy are hidden in your past. Trust what you perceive to be real.

MONDAY

WEEK 39

THE FABLE OF A WOMAN NAMED AUBERGINE

A mysterious woman called today.
(She called on the telephone and not in person.)
She is not a mystery woman you say?
She gave her name!
True, she did.
But the name was Aubergine and I know no woman named Aubergine.
Now who could this woman of mystery be?
Surely, now, you must know a woman named Aubergine!
No, no, no! I know no woman named Aubergine.
But, it would appear, this woman by the name of Aubergine
Is no quirk of fate.
It seems to me that it might well be that her name
Is not Aubergine at all.
And that she conceals another name:
A name she chooses to withhold.
We entertain this eve and the list is short:
For not but four have been asked.
And the woman named Aubergine is not of the list.
Yet a woman named Aubergine called
To confirm that she "would be there tonight".
Now, of the four invited, two are wed,
And two invited are unknown to each other:
One a man, the other a woman.
Surely, if the woman named Aubergine is the guest of the man,
She would have made this known.
So now a mysterious woman
Approaches our door.
A woman named Aubergine.
A woman who will be with us tonight.

First impressions: It's clear that something is coming to the person narrating this fable. We can see that they're trying to get an answer from a source that will not reveal what they want to know. In fact, the narrator already knows the answer. They just don't want to face the truth.

Set your intention for the week: This dramatic fable (one of three poems in this book written by my late mother) offers us the idea that things can never not have been. In essence, the future events suggested in this fable have happened already. This week, set your intention to notice that what is currently in your life is a direct result of where you were 90 days ago. Notice your spiritual germination time. What in your life right now did you begin thinking about in the past?

TUESDAY

COLOUR REFLECTION

What does Aubergine say to you? When we consider that Aubergine combines the blessing of the sixth sense with brown, which comes from the earth, we begin to see that our intuition is a real thing. There's a spiritual energy that purple always represents. In its highest calling Aubergine is an ability to harness your creativity and produce tangible results. Therefore, your intuitive impressions may also be real. In Aubergine we must be aware of how we harness our wisdom. Today, think about the times your intuition was correct and served you well.

WEDNESDAY

JOURNAL JOURNEY

Find your inspiration: One of the profound aspects of this fable – and of all the purple fables – is that in its present reality there's also a past. It's vital that we validate the reality we did endure of any trauma, pain or suffering from our family of origin.

It's easy to think that Aubergine could be a figment of the imagination. Many people live their lives denying their own reality. They suffer silently to protect themselves from seeing how unsafe their past really was.

When we risk knowing, we break through old fear-based beliefs and dispel the myth of "You are not to know". Things *are* as they seem. Trust that you are to know. In fact you know already, so today we'll take stock of how we allow others to invalidate us. Ask yourself the following questions, and then journal your answers:

- Am I willing to forgive myself for loving people who hurt or betrayed me?
- Even if I'm right, what do I really need to be free of my apprehension?
- What or who is my Aubergine?

THURSDAY

MAKE A CONNECTION

Connecting with yourself and others: These exercises are about seeking answers from the unknown. Just go with your chosen exercise, without trying to force a favourable outcome. What does it reveal to you?

Solo exercise: Think for a moment of something that you'd like an answer to. Now, with your eyes closed, flip through this book. Open it at random. What do you read? Is your answer there? Read between the lines. Your answer might be right in front of you.

Group exercise: In this exercise, everyone writes down on a slip of paper a life question they want answered. Toss all the papers in a hat. Each group member draws one (if you pick your own, put it back and take another). Now look at the question. Why did you draw it? Does it relate to you, too?

Now read the question aloud. Take a deep breath and answer as if you know what you're talking about - make something up, use your intuition. Have fun! Even if the answer seems wrong, it's important to say what's in your mind. By sharing something that you might not think applies to the situation, you may contribute a wise insight.

Are there others in the group who have answers? Allow them to offer their insight too. What is revealed?

FRIDAY

MEDITATION MOMENT

Going within: Aubergine is your own dread or internal fear. Now that you've met her, you have an opportunity to lessen her impact upon you. We use up a tremendous amount of spiritual energy on keeping our fears at bay. When these are cleared, this energy is released for us to use in intuitively seeking what will best support us.

MEDITATION

See yourself in a crystal-clear pool. As you wade in the water, a whirlpool swirls toward you and catches you. Aubergine is afraid you would leave if you weren't captive. Assure her that you will stay if she sets you free. She doesn't believe you; you are the first friend she's ever had. She doesn't want to be without you. You have met your own fear. Are you willing to be without her? Come to an agreement with her. (Perhaps she can help protect you from harm.) When she releases you, open your eyes. What is real? What is imagined? What is no longer necessary?

FAITH

Royal Purple Brick

This Week's Focus: I am more than I think I am.

MESSAGE OF THE WEEK

Being in the trance of a limiting belief can be such a powerful habit that it's locked into our muscle memory. This week we look at how we can physically manifest things in our lives to help us heal the wounds of our ancestry. Royal Purple Brick reminds us that we often cling to what we resist.

TORI'S TIP

The belief in a block is what keeps it in place. This week, keep in mind that the blocks in your life may no longer exist. Sometimes too much spiritual talk can keep you from actually living. If you've created physical ailments you may need professional help to clear them while you work on your body's memory of the block.

MONDAY WEEK 40

THE FABLE OF ROYAL PURPLE BRICK

Peggy couldn't see. A wall was preventing her from moving forward. What was going on? Why couldn't she get past? Finally, in terror, she cried out for help. A ray of Royal Purple light lit up the brick in her hands. She gasped. In the brick was a window into the heavens and there she could see the Council of the Great Spirits gathering.

The Great Goddess said, "She does not believe she'll survive if she lets go."

Sky God arrived, late as usual. "Why is this woman holding a brick?"

"She doesn't know that she is," the Great Servant replied.

"She thinks it's a wall," said Mother Earth.

Peggy looked at the Royal Purple Brick and the vibrant light flowing through her fingers. There was no wall! The path before her was missing one brick - the very one that she held in her hands.

When the council was gathered, the Great Servant spoke. "You've been in a trance of fear."

"I'm not trying to sabotage myself, if that's what you're implying," Peggy replied. In a huff, she threw the Royal Purple Brick onto the path before her.

Light exploded and the council appeared before her in a purple-hued hologram. "Are you ready to continue on your path?" Mother Earth asked.

"You cling to what you resist," Sky God added. "You'll do this again ..." A nudge from the Great Goddess silenced him.

"I don't understand," Peggy said.

The Great Servant stepped forward. Awed by his magnificent presence, Peggy took a step back. "You say you want greatness, but when it is offered you resist. You must be responsible for tearing down your own walls."

Peggy looked at the brick now back in place on her path. "I've put it down. Now what?"

"'Wait for inspiration," Mother Earth said. "It will come."

Sky God added, "You'll be isolated all your life if you keep doing this."

The Great Servant addressed the council. "The greatest gift we can give her is that of dignity. If this is how she wishes to die, then so be it."

"Wait!" Peggy shouted. "Don't leave me here."

"We must, child," said the Great Servant. "It is time."

"I don't want to leave this life yet. What should I do?"

"Move forward," said the Great Goddess. "No one knows what lies on the path ahead."

The Great Servant laughed. "Spirit exists in forward motion. We are always on the road ahead."

"Honour your life and you will teach others to honour theirs," came the words as the council disappeared into Royal Purple light. Peggy looked at the road ahead. There were many fine jewels in the path. This was going to be a colourful journey. Yes, indeed.

First impressions: Even when Peggy sees that she's holding the brick, she still resists the idea of letting it go. There's often a benefit of some kind when we refuse to let go of what no longer serves us. Holding that brick allows us to avoid taking responsibility. In the same way, we may hold our family of origin hostage - and keep the responsibility for our block outside ourselves.

Set your intention for the week: This week, think who in your family of origin you're still holding responsible for a particular situation in your life. For example, someone who finds relationships challenging may be holding their mother or father to blame. That way, when things don't work out, it's because of someone else's behaviour. This week, set an intention to see who's fault "it" really is.

TUESDAY
COLOUR REFLECTION

What does Royal Purple say to you? Royal Purple combines the communication of blue with the survival energy of red. Blue is about being bold and outspoken. In red our life-force meets our truth to create authenticity and give us the vitality to survive hard times. Use Royal Purple Brick to combine your energy with your spirit and deliver your message. If your problems seem magnified, perhaps you're too close to your difficulties. Take a step back to put things in perspective. Consider this: are you afraid of succeeding because it means that someone else will not be held responsible for their bad behaviour? If we fail then "they" never get off the hook, do they? Today, consider what it would be like to use the power of Royal Purple Brick to move past your self-imposed limits.

WEDNESDAY
JOURNAL JOURNEY

Find your inspiration: If this fable resonates with you, the fear of leaving your shelter and being abused may have grown so great that you no longer need a wall of fear to prevent you from living - a simple brick will do. The hope offered here is awareness. What we resist, we cannot heal.

Your fear may be holding you back, but fear may also indicate that you're trying to save yourself from a path that will not serve you. Are you following your true passion?

Be brave and let go of control. This fable promises freedom after surrender. Fear is always worse than the thing itself. Let go - the Great Spirits are there to catch you. It will be a life-changing experience for you. Accept the mystery. Release your Royal Purple Brick and be free.

Do you imagine that a wall has been built around you? The truth is that people can see right through the wall that you think is protecting you. This is the joke: everybody already knows what's up with you. Set an intention to relax if you're experiencing high levels of fear. In your journal, write to your fear. Ask it how it serves you. When it answers, acknowledge how valuable it has been for you. We never get rid of our fear, for it is our guardian, but we can renegotiate how it operates in our life. Ask fear to be your ally. What does it say?

THURSDAY

MAKE A CONNECTION

Connecting with yourself and others: It's important that you begin to give voice to what you've been holding on to. Try one of these exercises. Share your thoughts with someone you trust. If you're experiencing any physical pain, you may notice it starting to lift as you do this work.

Solo exercise: What's the one thing you're drawn to that's blocking your path? If weight loss is an issue, consider why you eat too much. How does it serve you? Just sit with your feelings about food. Can you write about them? Write in detail how it feels not to eat what you're drawn to. How does comfort food make you feel better? What can you substitute for it? Explore these questions and see where they take you. (You can substitute money, love or anything else for food.)

Group exercise: In this exercise, everyone takes turns admitting what they're unwilling to let go of that stops them going where they want. Next, each group member talks about someone else's issue as if it's their own (they're not giving advice) and imagines the steps they're going to take to put it down and move past it. Discuss the outcome as a group.

FRIDAY

MEDITATION MOMENT

Going within: Allow your soul to mingle with Spirit. As you journey through the Royal Purple light in this meditation, the Council of the Great Spirits may present themselves and give you information. Be open to them.

MEDITATION

Allow your whole self to emerge in Royal Purple light. Thank the child inside you for not letting others hurt you. Tell your inner child that as the adult you will now protect him or her and make choices for both of you. Allow your inner child to place the Royal Purple Brick where it belongs on the path and say another can be found along the road, should it be needed. The Royal Purple Brick is a part of your path, not the entire journey. Send the child off to play in the world, trusting that there are other colours beyond those that you both can presently see. Thank your guides for protecting you and not allowing you to give up.

GRATITUDE

Lucy from Indigo

This Week's Focus: I am so glad you are in my life.

MESSAGE OF THE WEEK

This week we look at the power of gratitude to fill us with love. While the fable is a simple letter to an unborn child from the mother's best friend, it also represents the unborn child in us all. Are you ready, are you willing, to allow yourself to live at this level of extraordinary gratitude?

TORI'S TIP

Love can come from unexpected sources. While some of us were born into challenging families, this fable is a reminder that someone somewhere loved us before we were even born. When we look at multi-generational healing, this idea becomes very important.

MONDAY WEEK 41

THE FABLE OF LUCY FROM INDIGO

Dear Baby

As you're not born yet, it's rather early for you to receive your first letter. But I wanted to give you something special. You have an extraordinary mother and I'd like to tell you about her. Where do I begin?

We perceive our mother as a parent. Through the growing years, mothers are the ones who send us to bed early, ask if our homework is done and tell us to brush our teeth and clean our room. As mothers have to take care of us, it can be hard to love and appreciate them while we're young. But sometimes, if we're lucky, we also see our mother as a friend.

All of us have at least one friend from the magical land of Indigo. Your mother Lucy is my friend from Indigo.

Lucy is rather shy. Well, humble. Lucy doesn't like to answer direct questions. She thinks certain things are private and she'd rather keep them to herself.

Sometimes I look at Lucy and love her so much.

What do I love about her?

I love her daring. I love her spirit. I love her intelligence. I love the way she bravely faces life. In short, I love the way she loves. She sees it all as a spiritual journey that we're making together. Lucy never planned to have this much love around her, but she does. She once said that she never saw herself getting married and having a family – and here she is expecting you.

I've never heard her utter a negative word. When I tell her of a problem, she always listens to what I have to say, then finds a moment to point out the good side. No matter what situation I'm in, she tells me that I'm receiving an opportunity. She smiles, gives me a hug, then tells me to hang in there. She encourages me to keep going and lets me know that things will work out.

She's not a quitter or a complainer. I complain, but not Lucy. Her smile sometimes says, "It's rough", but never, "I quit." She doesn't preach. I've never had a lecture from Lucy. You know what she feels by the look in her eyes – but you're never judged.

Lucy's love for me has taught me how to be a friend. Sometimes I wish I could be more like her, but she's never made me feel that being me is anything less than terrific.

The Great Spirits give each of us a friend from Indigo, someone who teaches us how to be a better friend. My friend's name is Lucy. I hope that someday your mother will be your friend from Indigo, too.

First impressions: On the surface this is a lovely letter to a friend's baby. But as we understand the power of Indigo, we can look deeper at the fable's meaning. Sometime in the future this unborn child will experience the ease of giving and receiving gratitude because they were infused with profound love before they were born. Our experience of family scarring can mask the energetic gifts that we've received.

Set your intention for the week: Think about the energetic gifts you've received from your family and others. Sometimes, if we've had a challenging childhood, we forget that there were those who helped us and made sure we survived. This week, set an intention to be grateful for the people who loved you, even though you might not have recognized that at the time.

TUESDAY

COLOUR REFLECTION

What does Indigo say to you? Indigo is one of the most powerful colours. Its combination of integrity and intuition brings a new perception to our lives. Indigo is a sacred warrior and gives a sense of spiritual protection. This is the colour of your third eye - your inner eye - and it offers wisdom and understanding. Lucy is from Indigo, which gives us a clue that the people of Indigo offer great service to others. Indigo people need structure in their lives; they tap into their intuition best when their world is safe. Aren't we all Indigo people? Today, reflect on what it would take for you to create a structure in your life whereby you can experience gratitude in a way that's profound and also suits you.

WEDNESDAY

JOURNAL JOURNEY

Find your inspiration: While Lucy from Indigo reminds us that friendship is a valuable asset, it's the deep Indigo gratitude from which the letter is written that holds the key to this fable. Be grateful for the people in your life. Are you unhappy in any of your relationships? Do you want something from someone - more love, perhaps? Remember that the feeling of love is in you, not something that you get from another person. It doesn't exist outside you.

The way to experience what you feel deprived of is to create it within. Lucy reminds us that when we change our emotional relationship to something, the external relationship will also change. In other words, if I'm filled with gratitude when I walk into a room, my experience is likely to be different from how it would be if I walk in filled with distress.

Lucy reminds us how to become the person we wish to be - we must simply be that person. Let go, live with gratitude and remember that kindness is contagious. If you treat anyone in your life badly, ultimately it's you who'll suffer the consequences.

How rich are you really? In your journal today, make a list of all your "assets" - the things in your life that you can be grateful for. Can you call on someone if you need them in the middle of the night? Is there food in your refrigerator? Have you received an invitation from a friend? Do you have good health? You're already the person you want to be. Be grateful.

THURSDAY
MAKE A CONNECTION

Connecting with yourself and others: In today's solo exercise, you reflect back on the person you admire most in your life. What qualities do they have that earns your admiration? Who do you need to be to possess those qualities - or do you, in fact, already have them? The group exercise was used to close the very first fable group I held. This is the original exercise; feel free to adapt it for your own group

Solo exercise: Pull out some paper and a pen. Write! Who is the person you admire most? Why? Who would you have to be in order to live at that level? Who is your mother? Who is your father? Are there any qualities you admire that they possess? If yes, what are they? If no, then think again. There's at least one quality they possess that you admire. Write about it. What kind of friend are you? Who is grateful for you?

Group exercise: Each person in the group has a magical gift for everyone. Take turns going around the circle, giving each group member the imaginary gift that you wish them to have. Whether you decide to give the gift of courage for facing a challenging situation or a magic hat that attracts romantic love, there's no limit to the imagination that you can express through this exercise. Take it wherever you want. Enjoy!

FRIDAY
MEDITATION MEANING

Going within: Making a daily gratitude list can be a meditative practice that brings peace and uplifts your emotional state. Meditation comes in many forms, the most important being those that brings you closer to Spirit. Allow yourself to be open to what works best for you.

MEDITATION

For the next ten days, spend a few minutes each day making a gratitude list. Do not look at the previous day's list when you begin each day and do not worry about coming up with new things to put down. At the end of ten days, read all the lists. Notice what keeps coming up. Are you on your list?

FORGIVENESS

Rhonda Rhino from Amethyst

This Week's Focus: We never forgive others, only ourselves for having judged them.

MESSAGE OF THE WEEK

This week we begin our journey into the meaning of forgiveness and we come to understand that the only real forgiveness is of ourselves.

TORI'S TIP

Rhonda is from Amethyst, just as Lucy is from Indigo. Amethyst signifies healing from addiction. Derivation - one's source - is important in spiritual discussion. As in all the fables that represent the intuitive third eye, there's an inherent sense of fairness and love in this story.

MONDAY — WEEK 42

THE FABLE OF RHONDA RHINO FROM AMETHYST

Rhonda was a quiet, good-tempered rhino who lived in the land of Amethyst. She was an only child and her mother, Delores, had a drinking problem. For a rhino coming of age that was hard to deal with. At gatherings her mother would stumble around, embarrassing Rhonda no end. She'd disappear for days at a time. Afterwards, Delores would have no recollection of these escapades, leaving Rhonda with the burden of shame for her mother's inexcusable behaviour.

Rhonda never blamed her mother. She longed for a quiet life. She wished every day that she could be the pet of a human child, with a place of her own to graze and sleep peacefully.

There were times when her mother was so drunk that she'd shout at Rhonda and accuse her of being spoiled. She called Rhonda's gentleness laziness, and her kindness weakness. For years, the mother berated the small rhino.

One day, hunters found the herd. Rhonda was grazing, unaware of the danger. Gunfire rang out and the rhinos scattered in all directions, a few falling to the ground.

As she ran through the forest, Rhonda spotted a human child standing transfixed in the path of the charging rhinos. A human female screamed in terror as Rhonda ran toward the child, scooped him up and carried him from danger. She was so scared, she'd no idea how far she ran or for how long. She stopped only when her hooves hurt so badly she could go no further.

The child cradled in her tusks was laughing and smiling at Rhonda. She gently lowered him to the ground and they stared at one another.

A tiny human hand came up and touched Rhonda's tough skin. She giggled and her new friend giggled too. They played together for a time, but as it grew dark the child began to cry.

Rhonda shook a tree to knock down some coconuts for the crying thing. He stopped and she watched him as he sipped his milk. She gathered some leaves into a pile and beckoned him to lie down. They curled up together and she warmed him through the long night.

At dawn humans came upon the sleeping duo. The sound of guns being cocked woke Rhonda. She didn't move, only looked up at the hunters as they took away her little boy. A shot rang out.

When she awoke, Rhonda was lying in a large garden. Her side was sore where the hunter's sleeping dart had hit her. A hand was touching her tusk. "Wake up, Rhonda," the little boy said. "We're home now."

Two larger humans were placing food on a picnic table. They smiled upon seeing Rhonda watching them.

"Come on Jeffrey. Bring Rhonda, it's time for dinner."

She sighed. It was a beautiful place. Her own yard, with a real family.

First impressions: Rhonda has a pure heart. She reminds us that what we don't take in, we don't have to work out. She offers us the idea that our choices can be based purely on love. No matter what happens to her, she never loses sight of her dream. Deprived of a loving home, her vision is to create one. Often our family patterns are revealed by what it is we desire most.

Set your intention for the week: This week, consider what has eluded you to this point, perhaps because of hidden family agreements. Set your intention to go where the love is and, like Rhonda, simply move away from conversations that don't bring out the best in you. Notice how this practice highlights what needs to be healed within.

TUESDAY
COLOUR REFLECTION

What does Amethyst say to you? Amethyst is a colour of higher consciousness. Its most pure, remarkable energy is all about healing. In the fable Rhonda is from Amethyst because this is the source of this energy. It's a purifying energy that transforms all that it connects with into a natural, loving state. Amethyst is a protector from a toxic situation and a powerful healer of addictions. Today, think what your life would be like if you could come from Amethyst, too.

WEDNESDAY
JOURNAL JOURNEY

Find your inspiration: Rhonda Rhino from Amethyst is all about forgiveness. As she doesn't take her mother's suffering personally, she's free to follow her dream. She's not bitter. There's a lightness to staying detached from another's anger and pain. Rhonda is the essence of goodness as she focuses on what she wants, not on what her mother did to her. In spirit, she transcends forgiveness because she never judges her mother. We only need to forgive if we've judged someone.

The actual circumstances of our life relate directly to what we focus on. Rhonda reminds us that if we focus on our dream with pure intention of heart, and forgive those who "trespass against us", miracles unfold.

Imagine that you have the energy of Rhonda Rhino. She holds no one accountable for her circumstances, nor does she complain about them. She doesn't express abandonment or abuse even though she has been abandoned and abused. In your journal today, describe who you'd have to let off the hook, so to speak, for you to be free. Write about why you don't want to let go. It's OK to feel that way; give yourself permission to be truthful. Don't worry about letting go, just notice how you feel. Think what you'd have to give up to embody Rhonda's freedom.

THURSDAY
MAKE A CONNECTION

Connecting with yourself and others: If you're not moving forward in an aspect of your life, there may be something you need to forgive yourself for. Gain awareness with one of these exercises.

Solo exercise: Is your habit of judging other people blocking you from achieving your dreams? What are you judging? Let's find out! Be the person you're judging. On paper, have them tell you what it's like to be dealing with you from their perspective. Sitting in their seat, wearing their life, how does it impact you to be them? Repeat all the excuses you've heard them say to you. Then defend their position. Take a few minutes to write to yourself explaining why that person has done what they've done. What new awareness do you have? Meditate with Rhonda Rhino for further guidance.

Group exercise: Ask someone in your group to pretend to be a person that you're still hard pressed to forgive. Sit opposite your fellow group member. Begin by explaining what has disappointed you. Now say what you need to hear to help you forgive. The other person, as best they can, will repeat back to you the exact words you need to hear. Now that you've heard those words, can you begin to forgive? Tell the other person how their actions have helped you. What have you learned? Discuss.

FRIDAY

MEDITATION MOMENT

Going within: Today, we focus on forgiving ourselves. Remember that people who seem truly nasty are usually that way in reaction to something, and also that all communication is either a cry for help or an offer of love. Come to this meditation with a desire to forgive. It's important to be willing to let go or it will not work for you. Light an amethyst candle and play some soothing music.

MEDITATION

Allow yourself to sink into the most innocent part of you. Breathe. Allow your mind's eye to see yourself living your dream. What is it you most desire? Take a few moments to experience your desire fully. Now, in the powerful healing light of Amethyst, bring forward someone you're struggling to forgive. Notice your reaction to them as you sit in the light of Amethyst. Ask yourself, "What deserves my energy - holding onto my dream or holding onto my resentment?" Allow your higher wisdom to guide you.

RECOVERY

The Lilac Key

This Week's Focus: Pain from our past unlocks the door of understanding.

MESSAGE OF THE WEEK

As we shift our focus to a new definition of recovery, we consider the idea of recovering a life that we've yet to live. Think about family ancestry and how that shows up in this fable to understand that your future success is hidden in your past.

TORI'S TIP

If we've suffered greatly in life, we may feel that happy memories or even our whole childhood has been taken away from us. Or we may be aware of something in our past holding us back, without being sure what it is. The promise of the Lilac Key is that if we face the painful memories we carry with us, they'll unlock the door of understanding to reveal the gifts hidden behind.

MONDAY WEEK 43

THE FABLE OF THE LILAC KEY

Greta woke in a cold sweat. She'd never forget that nightmare!

In her dream, she'd been a small child again, wandering through the streets around her old home. Once pristine, they were now littered and filthy. There was junk everywhere. She turned down her own street and stopped. At the end was a huge door, white light streaming through the keyhole.

She knew that she had to go through that door, that the key was somewhere in all the mess on the ground, but where? The voice of Mother Earth whispered to her, "Nothing is without purpose, little one. Everything is useful."

As she was gathering all the junk, some of it began abusing her (painful memories often do that). "You're a loser!" said one.

"My life was hard," said an old man's memory, "and you're just a stupid little girl."

"Get off me!" shouted another.

She gathered the pain and watched as it began taking shape in her hands.

"Brat!" hissed a fierce old secret, startling her.

When all the mess was gathered, Mother Earth sent heat to meld it together and Sky God cooled it with his wind. Before Greta's eyes the Great Lilac Key was formed.

She lifted the key and approached the door. When she placed it in the lock, a wave of fear washed over her. Pain enveloped her and agony rushed toward her like the wind. She was frightened, but she knew that she had to keep going in order to do more than merely survive.

She awoke just as the wind was beginning to die down and the pain starting to recede. It was over, only a dream. She shook off the bad memories and got out of bed.

Suddenly, there was a flash of light. She turned to see a door - the door from her dreams - slamming shut. Light streamed through the keyhole, as before. "It's still the dream," she told herself, backing away. She stumbled over something.

"Hey idiot," a secret growled at her.

She regained her balance. Her painful memories were strewn everywhere around the bedroom - somehow they'd got out! She knew what she must do. Greta began to gather her fears to unlock the door of understanding.

First impressions: Many people want to get rid of their pain, yet here we see that pain forms the foundation of our gifts. One of the most powerful insights of multi-generational healing is that we never lose our pain; rather we use it to empower us and add meaning to our lives.

Set your intention for the week: Think about the painful things in your life that you've wanted to get over. This week, set your intention to consider a new perspective - what if we never get over anything? What if painful experiences could become part of the magnificent tapestry of your life?

TUESDAY
COLOUR REFLECTION

What does Lilac say to you? Lilac offers the springlike energy of the first blush of love and the nurturing power of true friendship. This colour mingles the otherworldly essence of deep purple with the white light of detachment that allows us to see the bigger picture. In its most pure form Lilac is about expressing yourself through co-operation with Spirit. Your spirit guides come forth in Lilac and offer divine guidance. The promise of Lilac is this: no matter what challenges lie ahead, you'll have the support you need to face them. Today, become aware of your inner strength and also of the strength of your friends and community, who are there to assist you if the need arises.

WEDNESDAY
JOURNAL JOURNEY

Find your inspiration: Change is coming and can't be avoided. You may be tempted to try to run away from this situation, but it's a necessary challenge for you. You're going through the pains of birth and they may be short-lived like a lilac's flowers or last for a long time as do a lilac tree's roots. Whether you're enduring a divorce, the bitter ending of a business partnership or some other difficult circumstance, Lilac represents the death of an old way of living, thinking and surviving - and the birth of a new one.

The fable of the Lilac Key tells you that mere survival is no longer enough for you. Your will to live is forcing change. This is a change of consciousness, which in turn will lead to the restoring of balance and harmony in all areas of your life. Cleaning up the past is often painful, but from this process come hope and joy.

Remember, once the key has been used to open the door, once you've entered this new consciousness, you can't go back. Get ready; there may be a sudden jolt and change will come. This is a new dawn and it represents the ending of denial. Today in your journal, recall a challenging time in your past and remind yourself what it took for you to walk through it and come out the other side. When you've finished, look at what you've written as a roadmap of how to face such difficult circumstances again. You've now created a new tool for your spiritual toolkit.

THURSDAY
MAKE A CONNECTION

Connecting with yourself and others: In the solo exercise, you'll use automatic writing to bring forward a set of circumstances or a person that you feel has taken something from you. This can be a very powerful healing tool. The group activity introduces using the *Chakra Wisdom Oracle Cards*. If you don't have the deck, you can access the cards for free online.

Solo exercise: Identify an individual, a group or an event in your past that you feel has taken something from you. In your journal, start a dialogue between yourself and this other person or situation. Without thinking about what you're writing, describe your issue with this person or situation and ask them what they suggest you should do. Allow the other party to respond to you, on paper, and let them be the voice of reason and tell you how to solve this problem. Stay with this process through to completion. Trust that you'll know when you're finished by a shift in your energy. Be open to choices other than those you thought you knew already.

Group exercise: This exercise uses the *Chakra Wisdom Oracle Cards*. Each group member picks a card and uses the single-word name of the card as their guide (this is the same keyword given to each fable in this book). How does this one word unlock the truth of what's going on? How does it open the door of understanding for each person? Discuss. If you seek more understanding about recovery, pick another card with that question in mind. The card you choose will help you find the path of recovery. If you don't have the deck, you can use the free random shuffler on my website: www.ChakraWisdomOracle.com

---

FRIDAY

MEDITATION MOMENT

Going within: What do you choose to see in your meditation? How does your vision differ today from what you'd have chosen a year ago? Stepping into your future, would what you see be any different? Why or why not?

MEDITATION

Imagine standing outside a door, holding a string of keys. Each key is a different chakra colour. One key calls out to you. Visualize opening the door with it. Let the light from the other side wash over you as you enter. Is the light a particular colour? What do you see? You can go with what you see first or create anything you like. Are there people you'd like to meet? A home you'd like to live in? The perfect job? Or simply seeing yourself walking in serenity? Have fun! Allow yourself this new existence. What is this journey about?

BALANCE

Emaciated Periwinkle

This Week's Focus: I must create before the opportunity disappears.

MESSAGE OF THE WEEK

There's a sense of urgency to this fable. Periwinkle is sure that the life he could have is better then the life he has. He gives up the support and love of the people around him for the sake of a fantasy. He's not yet developed his craft, yet he naïvely thinks that he's ready to step into the limelight.

TORI'S TIP

Remember that nothing happens by accident. The circumstances in which you find yourself are those you created, just as Periwinkle is responsible for abandoning the people who helped him get the opportunity to live his dream. Periwinkle lacks emotional maturity. Notice how this may resonate for you.

MONDAY

WEEK 44

THE FABLE OF EMACIATED PERIWINKLE

Once upon a time in the land of Hectic, there lived a sparkling youth named Periwinkle. He'd often break into song and dance to amuse his friends. He drew pictures for the youngsters and even entertained at their birthday parties. The town adored him and believed him to be a special talent.

One day, a theatre agent was visiting her friend Mrs Gold, the owner of the Hectic Playhouse. Mrs Gold told her friend of the town's pride, Periwinkle. The agent was always scouting for new talent and was eager to meet this young man.

The agent asked Periwinkle to prepare an audition piece and come to her office in nearby Starville in one month's time. So Periwinkle dropped everything. He barely slept. He practised his piece day and night. He failed to show up at little Percy's birthday party because he wanted to rehearse. Percy was in tears and the party was a disaster.

Periwinkle stopped eating. "Takes too much time. Besides, I'm really not hungry."

He stopped returning his phone calls. One was from Mrs Gold. A few days later he ran into her in the street. "Periwinkle!" she called out, "I'd love to have you do a part in our new ..."

He gestured in the way he'd seen great actors do; he was sure he was on his way to becoming one himself. "No, Mrs Gold, I can't do your little theatre anymore. I'm on my way to the big time."

"I understand," said Mrs Gold, but she was surprised - and hurt. She loved the Hectic Playhouse. She thought it *was* the big time. She wasn't going to call that boy again!

In a month Periwinkle managed to alienate everyone he knew. The night before his big audition, he was frantic and couldn't sleep. He called his best friend, Purple. When Purple heard Periwinkle's voice, he huffed, "I'm too busy for you!" Then he hung up.

"But he's never too busy for me." Periwinkle's brow wrinkled up. "Well, who care what anyone thinks. I'm going to be a big star after tomorrow."

The audition was a success. The agent told Periwinkle he was excellent - that he offered quite a bit of promise. She asked him to sign a contract with her agency.

As his pen glided across the paper he asked, "Now what happens?"

"Well, we wait," she said.

"For what?" Periwinkle stopped writing.

"For the right job to come along. I have to wait for jobs to come in and then I send you on auditions. So go home and I'll call you when something happens."

"Oh," he said, trying hard to hide his disappointment. "I thought you had jobs. I mean ..."

"It takes time," said his new agent. "For now, just keep doing what you're doing."

He was getting nervous. "Well, I'm not really doing that anymore ..."

She put his contract in a folder. "This business is no different than any other, it's all about relationships. If people like you, then you'll do well. Keep up the good work!"

Periwinkle shook her hand, feeling glum. On his way home, he thought about all the relationships he was going to have to repair. The question he kept asking himself was, "How did I let things get so out of balance?"

First impressions: It's a mistake to assume that life will be instantly transformed once we get what we want. When a much-anticipated event actually happens, how do you experience it? Do you ignore those who've been there for you or do you celebrate with them?

Set your intention for the week: At the end of the fable, Periwinkle realizes that he must go home and repair his friendships. He does this not to further his career, but to regain his happiness. This week, think about the part of you that would give up everything for a dream. Set your intention to start thinking about ways of incorporating that dream into your life.

TUESDAY

COLOUR REFLECTION

What does Periwinkle say to you? Periwinkle combines the impartial energy of grey, the honesty of blue and the spirituality of purple. It gives the ability to listen without stating an opinion or taking a stand. It tells others that you're content simply to exist as a spiritual entity, and that you offer balance and calm. All the purple fables have brought you to this point. Today, take some time to think about the aspects of your life that may be out of balance. Are there any signs warning you of this? Periwinkle reveals the causes of disharmony in the world.

WEDNESDAY

JOURNAL JOURNEY

Find your inspiration: If Periwinkle has stirred you, it's a good indication that something in your life is out of balance. If you focus too much on one area, you risk neglecting another. Remember that change takes place in its proper time. Slow down. With balance we gain the love and support we need for taking necessary risks.

Periwinkle reminds you to look at your eating habits. Be watchful of your diet and listen to your body if it's asking you to take better care of yourself. Just because Periwinkle is out of balance doesn't mean you need to be, too. When you're planning an important change in your life, don't forget to take care of your physical well-being. Don't take on too much at once.

Are you addicted to work or do you have any other compulsive behaviour patterns? Is there a part of your life that needs serious attention?

Periwinkle brings up the idea of wanting to escape into a new life. Today, write in your journal why you'd like to do this. Then ask your angels to join you and guide your pen as you answer this question: "How can I escape into the life I currently have?"

THURSDAY

MAKE A CONNECTION

Connecting with yourself and others: Is there an area in your life that feels out of balance? What are the obstacles to overcome in resolving your problem? For example, perhaps your job has taken over your life and you want to leave it, but you also have a commitment to supporting your family. Choose one of these exercises to discover a way forward.

Solo exercise: Using your intuition, write down the name of someone with whom you don't have a balanced relationship. Now write down a few creative ways to reconnect with that person. The point of the exercise is to allow ideas in without censorship. Stay open to these questions: "How have I gained by this imbalance? How would healing and repairing the imbalance support me in moving forward?" If you choose yourself as the person you're out of balance with, what do you see in your answers?

Group exercise: Describe to your group what you think a balanced life is. Are you out of balance in one area of your life? Imagine that you're now two months in the future. In the area of your life that was a challenge, you've achieved balance. Finally! Take a few minutes to tell the group how you did this. How is your life different? Make sure that you tell everyone what your current situation looks and feels like. If you can imagine it, you can have it. Would you like it? Ask the group for input on taking the first steps toward finding balance in your life.

FRIDAY

MEDITATION MOMENT

Going within: The truth is that we must be willing to live with being out of balance, because our lives are in constant motion. Balance is never still. When things are in flow, they're not stagnant.

MEDITATION

Relax. Relax. Relax. Look at Periwinkle. So skinny. So lonely. Think about what you feel is missing in your life, if anything. Journey with Periwinkle. He tells you of the work he had to do to repair past mistakes. He says: "We all end up in the same place, so enjoy your journey." Sit with him. You will know when it is time to come back.

IMPARTIALITY

Bahana Beige

This Week's Focus: I quietly listen, allowing you to colour your own palate.

MESSAGE OF THE WEEK

This week, as we enter the neutral chakra, we focus on the concept of impartiality. Over the next few days, whenever you encounter resistance in your life, take a moment to argue for the opposition. In other words, take a stand for the views that are against your own. To really understand a situation, you need to listen openly to the other side.

TORI'S TIP

The key here is self-discipline. Being neutral requires strength and a lot of personal energy. It's much easier sometimes to jump right in and try to figure out a situation immediately rather than wait calmly for the participants to resolve it themselves.

MONDAY WEEK 45

THE FABLE OF BAHANA BEIGE

The town of Beige was not like many small towns, for it had a dictator. While dictators in general are not known for bringing peace and harmony, Beige's ruler Bahana was. Bahana Beige knew that to truly be a leader, you must listen. Representatives of other towns often came to seek the counsel of the wise dictator of Beige.

There was no crime in the town of Beige, not until the day Mr Grey stole some clothes that had been hung out to dry outside the Yellow family's house.

Bahana Beige called on Mr Grey. "What's the matter?" she gently inquired.

Mr Grey explained that he couldn't afford to clothe his family and the Yellows wouldn't miss what he'd taken.

"How can we resolve this?" Bahana asked.

"I could return the things and apologise." He sighed. "That doesn't really solve my problem though."

Bahana listened patiently.

"I still need clothes for my family. Maybe I could ask the Yellows for help to get us through this time."

Her soft fingers touched his hand. "You're on the right track. Let me know what happens." She left, trusting that Mr Grey would do the right thing.

Not long after, the Smiths moved into Beige. They complained about everything and everyone. They hadn't been in Beige very long before Mr Smith demanded an audience with Bahana Beige about what he said was a serious situation with his neighbour, Mrs Stanton.

Mr Smith and Mrs Stanton couldn't agree what colour the fence dividing their property should be painted. Bahana listened to them quietly for a while. Soon Mrs Stanton and Mr Smith were so taken up with shouting loudly at each other that they didn't notice Bahana slip out of the room. On her return she presented each of them with a can of paint.

They looked at the cans. "There must be some mistake," they both said. She'd given each of them the colour the other had chosen.

"How so?" she asked. "Opinions are like fences. We build them only to protect ourselves from each other. You'll paint your fence the colour chosen by your neighbour. When you can see the colour of one another's world, you'll have understanding. Always take the other side before your own and you'll remain peaceful."

First impressions: Rarely do we trust others to put themselves back on track without interference. In this fable we discover what it means to be a conduit of Spirit: remaining involved with others but remaining open to them finding their own solutions.

Set your intention for the week: This fable outlines the difference between sympathy and empathy. When we sympathize, we often become emotionally involved and offer advice. Sympathy implies that the other person doesn't know how to handle their problems and needs us. When we empathize, we empower the other person by supporting them in their feelings, trusting that they have everything they need to solve their own challenges. This week, notice whether you're offering advice or support to others. Set your intention to observe how empowered people feel when you empathize rather than advise.

TUESDAY

COLOUR REFLECTION

What does Beige say to you? Beige blends into the background, allowing other colours to be dominant. It's a true neutral, blending peacefully without standing out and enhancing the appearance of the colours around it. The essence of Beige is to augment other colours. What a marvellous gift! As you contemplate Beige now, take a few minutes to think about how *you* uplift the lives of others. Beige speaks of dependability. Conservative in nature, it holds the truest of values but reserves opinion. Like all the neutral colours, it brings forward the highest calling of one aspect of your spiritual life. Beige is flexible and willing to listen to other people's opinions. Today, ask yourself: "Am I open to other points of view? Can I listen with impartiality no matter what's being said?"

WEDNESDAY

JOURNAL JOURNEY

Find your inspiration: If you're drawn to Bahana Beige, it's time to take an impartial look at your situation and drop the excuses. Listen. Your answers will come when you remain still.

You may gain valuable insight by looking at your circumstances from another perspective. If you're challenged in a relationship with someone, try seeing things from that person's point of view. Approaching an argument from the other side greatly improves communication. When we're fixed on a position or an opinion, we're not in the neutral space that this fable describes.

This is an opportunity to see who you are in a relationship. Ask yourself, "How does my present attitude or position serve me?" When you answer this question, you'll gain more insight into choosing a path for the highest good. Remember, this isn't a time of action, but a time of reflection. Today, take some time to write in your journal about the new ideas that have come to you from Bahana Beige.

THURSDAY

MAKE A CONNECTION

Connecting with yourself and others: These exercises are about taking stock of your life. Focus on working with the energy of Bahana Beige.

Solo exercise: Can you take an impartial view of who you are? Looking at your life as a neutral observer, take a moment to answer what's working well in this person's life - and what isn't. Consult with Bahana and list at least five things in each category. Any there any pleasant surprises?

Group exercise: Take turns to discuss a person or situation that's truly aggravating you. Say what's on your mind but don't dwell on it - just spend a few minutes on this part of the exercise. Then take a moment to relax and release the situation from your body. When you're ready, allow your group to give you feedback on what you can do. Be aware of having a negative reaction to this feedback ("I've already thought of that!"). Let the group discuss which of the various choices available to you in the present situation is for the highest good. What's the grace of the situation? How has this been a powerful teacher for you? What would Bahana Beige say? Hint: Always choose *love*.

FRIDAY

MEDITATION MOMENT

Going within: This meditation is about journeying with Bahana Beige in order to experience the deep compassion of impartiality. Can you hold deep love for another, without passing judgment on them or their circumstances?

MEDITATION

Imagine a mist forming. Bahana Beige beckons you into the mist. When you are ready, allow her energy and knowledge in. You may or may not receive a message. If something happens, then allow it to happen, but you are to follow, not lead. Nothingness is the goal. Clarity comes when the mist clears. Open your eyes when you are ready and thank Bahana for reminding you to be with yourself.

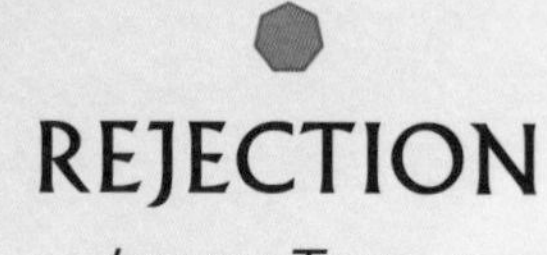

REJECTION

Ivory Tower

This Week's Focus: They won't use me.

MESSAGE OF THE WEEK

This is the final poem of three in this book by my late mother. She made these observations in 1958, using a gay artist as a metaphor for the person who doesn't conform. This week, we consider the cost of being an individual.

TORI'S TIP

This story has two powerful, opposing interpretations. One is about society's rejection of the artist for not conforming. The other is about self-imposed exile and the artist's need to protect his identity and not give up who he is. In fact, both artist and society are rejecting each other. Through this fable, we discover the importance of protecting your personal gifts.

MONDAY

WEEK 46

THE FABLE OF IVORY TOWER

They called me for jury duty.
But they won't use me.
I have a beard.
I paint pictures nobody understands.
They won't use me.
I have intelligence; I know moderation.
I could lecture on the aesthetic principles.
I have a great deal to say.
I paint because it is the only way I can say it.
People interest me.
But that's it; they interest me.
If I didn't put all my time into painting,
I'd try to understand them.
But I don't have another lifetime,
And I can't make it this time.
I can't seem to feel any sympathy.
My life is with theory,
And while there are times
That people give me pause to think,
I don't pause long enough I guess,
Because when I'm done, I come up with nothing.
I'm neutral, I guess.
They call me for jury duty
Once in every four years.
I go through with it.
I know what they'll ask and what they think
When they're writing down the answers.
They won't use me.
They want someone with emotion.
I have to save that emotion for my painting.
I can't tell them that.
They want somebody who will put himself
In the other guy's place. I can't do that.
I'd never be in that guy's place.
I walk away from trouble.
I never get mixed up with anything
Or anyone. They honour my individuality
When they invite me, yet when I appear
They deny that individuality
Because they won't use me.
Maybe they need me for the balance,
If only to put them into a spin for a while.
If only to show them that the world is also
Homosexual, artistic, solitary, indefinite,
Arbitrary, insecure and pathological.
It would give them something to think about.
And it would give me something to think about.

First impressions: At first glance the fable appears to be about being rejected. However, the artist is resigned to the idea that the court won't use him. In fact, he's never really rejected, because he's invited and he continually does his part. Although he's highly aware of the limitations of others, the artist continues to show up because, as he states at the end of the fable, he hopes that his contribution opens the conversation of new thought around old ideas.

Set your intention for the week: Is there something that you feel you've been excluded from? A place where you feel you don't belong? Ask yourself: "Did I really want to be part of that anyway?" This week, set your intention to become aware of where you feel slighted in life, and to open yourself to love and tolerance of those who are different from you.

TUESDAY
COLOUR REFLECTION

What does Ivory say to you? White is about enlightenment, but the pure, warm energy of Ivory opens the idea of self-focus. It represents a softening toward others and an absorption of things that are outside oneself. This colour is about being self-aware and tells others that you have knowledge of yourself. White deflects but Ivory begins the journey of allowing others into your life, in small but important steps. Today, inspired by Ivory, think of an area of your life in which you feel secretly afraid or insecure. Is there someone who you can tell your secret to? If you can, do so.

WEDNESDAY
JOURNAL JOURNEY

Find your inspiration: The Ivory Tower reflects how you function when the world seems to have values that are different from your own. You may feel that you don't fit into the world as it is, but by focusing on the differences between the world and you, you may realize that these differences also benefit you on some level.

There are times when you must sacrifice being like everyone else in order to be true to yourself. This is the message of the Ivory Tower. If you're considering moving away from the norm, don't worry about being unhappy. As the artist chooses to express himself with paint, you too must express yourself, even if that means that "they" won't want you. As in the Ivory Tower, rejection is the Great Spirits' way of protecting us.

This fable symbolizes inner wisdom and personal strength. It's about reaching out as who you are. Whether or not you're accepted you must follow your path. No matter what may be facing you, don't lose your integrity. When you least expect it, a supportive teacher or mentor may be sent to you by the Great Spirits. Perhaps this person will not be someone you would have picked. Don't judge by outer appearances.

Have there been times when you've taken part in something even though you're unlikely to win? Journal about that experience and about why you showed up anyway – was there a win in it for you after all? Write down what it's like when you take the high road.

THURSDAY
MAKE A CONNECTION

Connecting with yourself and others: The solo exercise allows you to notice labels that may have been stuck on you as a child. Are they true? If not, find better ones. The group exercise explores how who you are is closely linked to the ways you're similar to and different from the people in your life.

Solo exercise: On separate pieces of paper, write down any labels you've been given in your life. Pick up one label at a time and note down how that label has affected your life. Is this label true? If it's true, what would make it untrue? Note down any beliefs you've adopted about yourself because of this old label. Now come up with new labels to replace those that have hindered your growth. With your new labels to empower you, take a few minutes to write down all the ways these new labels are going to change your life.

Group exercise: Write down who you are on a piece of paper. Keep it brief. Touch on these three areas: how you connect with others; what makes you stand out; and what makes you blend in. Share this with your group. Allow others to notice how this list might fit them as well. Are you beginning to see the partnership you share with those you choose to be close to? How do you want to express yourself in the world? What have you discovered? Discuss.

FRIDAY

MEDITATION MOMENT

Going within: The Ivory Tower is your safest place. It's your place of creation and fulfilment. When you go into the Ivory Tower and find your way home, you can safely create your own world. What you manifest here can change your life for ever.

MEDITATION

Imagine divine Ivory light filtering down and encircling you. In the distance, the Ivory Tower beckons. You reach the castle and the drawbridge slowly lowers. You enter the castle grounds and come to the tower. At the top of the stairs is a door. You enter a room with windows all around, the beautiful afternoon light streaming in. This is a safe place, the place of no judgment. Here you can set up your easel. What picture would you paint? Go to a window and look out. What do you see? This is the perfect place to contemplate the life before you. You've finally found your way home.

RELEASE

Shadow Grey Storm

This Week's Focus: I can no longer keep your secrets.

MESSAGE OF THE WEEK

This week, we become aware that the universe is only holding up a mirror and showing us who we are. There's no judgment and there can be no hiding. This fable isn't about our secrets being revealed, but about finally seeing who we really are.

TORI'S TIP

In many ways Shadow Grey Storm is the part of you that desperately wants someone else to take responsibility for your circumstances. Shadow appears to allow you to see that the people you judge may have evolved past whatever it is you're still judging them for. The lesson here is that nothing is inherently bad or wrong; we need to reinterpret what has occurred in our life.

MONDAY

WEEK 47

THE FABLE OF SHADOW GREY STORM

The rain spat in Nikita's face as she rushed home through the dark, empty streets. Her mother had reminded her to take an umbrella, but she tried not to listen to her mother, who'd never liked her. She'd told Nikita so often enough. Nikita would never amount to anything, she'd told her. But then her mother had said so many nasty things.

As Nikita forged through the storm, her thoughts shot ahead to the scene waiting for her at home. No doubt there would be hot soup waiting on the table. "She's always trying to make everything she did to me OK. Well, it's not!" Nikita didn't want anything from her mother any more. She wasn't going to eat the stupid soup.

She rounded a corner and a large grey shadow blocked her path. Terrified, she turned and fled. The shortest way home was through the graveyard. She ran until her heart was pounding so hard she couldn't take another step. When she stopped, gasping for air, she was surrounded by tombstones. Her nervousness forced laughter out of her.

The large shadow she'd been running from appeared before her.

"Go away!" Nikita screamed. She'd read once that a spirit would leave if you commanded it to do so.

It didn't work. The shadow sat down. Shadows don't really sit, of course, but that's what it looked like. Nikita was half-blinded by the rain, but the shadow seemed oddly familiar.

"Why are you here?" she demanded.

"I don't care what you say, it's all your fault," the shadow said. "I'm never going to forgive any of you. I'd rather rot here."

Nikita grew pale. She recognized the voice. It was her own.

"Why me?" the shadow wailed.

Although she desperately wanted the voice to stop, Nikita knew that she must listen. She heard herself abandon others. She heard herself promise to never forgive those who loved her. She heard how she'd made herself miserable.

Shadow Grey Storm never speaks any words other than our own. When Shadow Grey Storm had uttered the final word, the rain stopped. Dawn was breaking. Nikita wiped the tears from her eyes and looked around her with new vision. Shadow Grey Storm mingled with the grey mist of morning and disappeared. The sun began to shine as she stood to leave the graveyard.

"It's going to be a beautiful day," Nikita thought. "It's going to be my day!"

When she arrived home, her mother was still awake. The old woman was worried sick. For the first time ever, Nikita comforted the frail woman who'd once been so harsh to her.

That was the morning that Nikita met herself and forgave her mother. She also forgave herself for loving her mother all along. Soon after the visit from Shadow Grey Storm, Nikita moved out of her mother's house. For the very first time she was on her own. Her anger had moved out, too. She felt safe.

First impressions: Nikita kept herself chained to her past, even though her circumstances had changed and her mother was no longer the abusive person she'd once been. When Nikita realizes that she herself is perpetuating her own inner torment, she's able to forgive herself for loving someone who has hurt her.

Set your intention for the week: What would your world look like if you took things at face value? What if, for one week, you allowed yourself to see the best in others? Can you see how the people you've had challenging relationships with have grown? This week, set your intention to let go of the story you think you know and accept people at face value.

TUESDAY

COLOUR REFLECTION

What does Grey say to you? Grey combines the enlightenment of White with the seriousness of Black. It reminds us that we must engage with the unknown and speaks of a power that we've yet to understand. Grey remains neutral to all that challenges it; there's no judgment, only respect. This colour makes us stop and in its shadows we can see the true nature of our being. Today, think about what a grey day is. While some people may feel that's a depressing idea, others celebrate the neutral environment of grey. Allow yourself to be the observer today; let contemplation be your guide. Release emotion and be completely present with others.

WEDNESDAY

JOURNAL JOURNEY

Find your inspiration: Shadow Grey Storm holds our deepest secrets. When it appears, it's because we can't move forward in our lives without first facing our own fears. Shadow Grey Storm doesn't judge our secrets; it simply mirrors who we are.

This fable is about taking responsibility and not blaming others for your situation. If Shadow Grey Storm appeals to you, it could be that you need to confront an unresolved issue that's buried in your past. Shadow Grey Storm is an inevitable awakening, by conscious choice or not. You can't hide and move forward at the same time. Whether meeting Shadow Grey Storm is a pleasant experience or not, you, like Nikita, will feel a refreshing release from your bonds.

The shame of a secret may stifle us. The rays of light in this fable's illustration (see page 198) represent piercing knowledge and hidden truth. Today, investigate in your journal the idea of secrets that have held you back. What are your secrets? What would it take for you to release them? What's the worst thing that could happen if you did so? Staying neutral, answer these questions. Facing your own shadow is empowering. What does your shadow tell you?

THURSDAY

MAKE A CONNECTION

Connecting with yourself and others: This week's exercises help you to explore your buried resentment. Only do the group exercise with people you feel safe with.

Solo exercise: Write down a resentment that you're holding on to. What would it take for you to let go and move forward? If you don't know, guess. The Council of the Great Spirits is convening right now. The Great Spirits know what you need to do and are willing to help you. Are you ready? Write down the minutes of their meeting. What wisdom do they have about your situation?

Group exercise: Choose a few group members to play the roles of you and your immediate family. Place them in a scene according to your impression of your relationship with them and their relationship with each other. Are they seated or standing? Are they facing one another or turned away? Place your parents first, then your siblings, then the person playing you. Give each person a statement, such as "It's all too much for me", or, "I've got to make more money." As you observe, each person in turn says their statement, getting louder and louder until it becomes too much. Pause and share. Now speak to one person. Tell them whatever you need to. What do you need to hear from them? You may talk to more than one person if you wish. To finish, each participant states, "My name is ______ and I am not the role I played."

FRIDAY

MEDITATION MOMENT

Going within: To gain the wisdom of Shadow Grey Storm, you must be willing to listen to yourself. Today, take some time to be still in your own company and just listen.

MEDITATION

To do this meditation, you must have no distractions. Shadow Grey Storm simply asks that you sit and listen. In the silence you will hear yourself. If you sincerely seek freedom, Shadow Grey Storm may come to you.

INSTINCT

Wolf of White Light

This Week's Focus: There is a guide inside us.

MESSAGE OF THE WEEK

There's a real magic when we work with our gut instinct in the seventh chakra. This week is a chance to look at how you use your instinct to make meaning of circumstances and to create thoughts and even things in your world. Ultimately, this fable is about being guided by Spirit.

TORI'S TIP

The Wolf is warrior energy. He protects, endures harsh conditions and survives. He represents the power of the human spirit. We love Wolf because he taps into the survivor in us all. His message is to look forward, not backward. The risk in looking behind us is that we'll miss what's right in front of us.

MONDAY

WEEK 48

THE FABLE OF WOLF OF WHITE LIGHT

The Wolf of White Light climbs the treacherous rocks unseen, his eyes always fixed on the high ground ahead.

During the time he prepared to be a guardian, his master trained him never to turn back.

"When we look behind, we sap the energy we are to use in the future. If the Great Servant had wished us to look behind, he would have given us eyes in the back of our heads," his master said.

His defence is his instinct and he would sense danger. Hence the Wolf of White Light journeys on and does not look below for his enemies. He carries on, for the Council of the Great Spirits lies on the road ahead.

He climbs unseen, for only those who seek a spirit guide can see him.

First impressions: As the shortest fable of all, the Wolf of White Light reminds us that brevity may be required at this time. His story is simple. He is warrior energy and warriors don't tell their stories, they live them. When the Wolf appears, it's time to look at the protective mechanisms that you've set up in your life, which may be keeping people away from you. Like a guard protecting an armoury that's no longer needed, the Wolf may represent an aspect of your self-protection that you need to reassign.

Set your intention for the week: This week, take a look at what you conceal from others. Wolf energy is often created by a wounded inner child. This protective mechanism, while important at the time, may now be operating in overdrive. This week, set your intention to look at the coping devices that no longer work for you. Don't attempt to get rid of Wolf, but instead use him to support you in a new endeavour.

TUESDAY

COLOUR REFLECTION

What does White say to you? White is the colour of purity and enlightenment. Although the other colours are attracted to it, White has a masculine energy that deflects colour, protecting the pure core from contamination and allowing nothing in. White insulates your thinking and protects it. It may be that you shouldn't allow anything to get in the way of your journey. What you've embarked upon must be completed. Today, consider what it would take for you to trust that your spirit guide is on the path just ahead, beckoning you. Allow white light to surround you if any doubts or fear come up. Notice how this powerful energy is alive all around you.

WEDNESDAY

JOURNAL JOURNEY

Find your inspiration: The Wolf of White Light reminds you that you must use your instinct, for that's what protects you. You're more aware than you realize.

Wolf warns that time spent in the past leaves you defenceless in the present and that focusing on past injustices will not prepare you for the future. If you don't let go of the old, you may miss the opportunities that the Great Spirits plan to offer you.

This is the spirit guide that comes to lead you up the mountain you need to climb. Allow him to guide you. If this fable resonates with you, the time has come to move on. With your eyes focused on where you're heading, you may see the Wolf of White Light waiting in the distance for you. Now is the time to act.

You may find it necessary to shed some of your load, allowing you to travel light. Today, write down in your journal any obtrusive thoughts that get in the way of your progress - about perceived past injustices, for example. Really allow yourself to write out any anger, upset or displeasure with the way things are or have been. Giving your obsession to Spirit in the form of writing will lighten your load for the journey ahead. Write until there's nothing left and you feel your energy shift.

THURSDAY

MAKE A CONNECTION

Connecting with yourself and others: The Wolf of White Light is here to guide you to Spirit. Choose an exercise today to help you step forward in the knowledge of who you really are.

Solo exercise: Sometimes, living authentically is more about what we remove from life than about what we add to it. What needs to be removed from your life? What does your gut tell you? Spend some time writing about something that's in your way and commit to letting it go. Use your inner knowledge as your guide and listen out for feedback from the universe about how to do this.

Group exercise: This is one of the most powerful exercises I use and I do it in almost every group I lead. It's often the most popular and fun, not to mention eye-opening! You'll need a timer. Play in teams of two and sit facing each another. Imagine that it's now one year from today's date. While one person listens and takes notes, the other person talks for three minutes about all that has happened to them in the past year - personally, professionally, health-wise, holiday-wise - anything they can think of. When the three minutes are up, switch roles. When you've finished, take a few minutes to share any observations you may have about the experience.

What you've done in essence in this exercise is lay out the path ahead for the coming year. The Wolf of White Light journeys ahead on the path you've set out before you. Follow him; he is your guide. Call to him when you lose your way.

FRIDAY

MEDITATION MEANING

Going within: In this meditation, you journey along an imaginary trail with the Wolf of White Light. Be aware of all of the emotions that come up during the meditation. If you write them down afterwards, your notes may help you identify the road ahead. Don't judge or reject anything you see but be open to new ideas. It may be helpful to play a piece of soothing music as you journey.

MEDITATION

Imagine a waterfall of light washing down from above. Allow it to splash over you until you feel completely relaxed. The Wolf of White Light beckons to you. Go. As he guides you, what do you see? Does he talk to you? He may not; communication takes many forms. Is he friendly? Neutral? Do you have any innate knowledge about him? If he allows it, look into his eyes. Previously unseen sights may now be revealed to you. When it is time to return, the Wolf of White Light will lead you back to the path. Trust him, he is your instinct.

DESTINY

Black and White

This Week's Focus: Together we are stronger than alone.

MESSAGE OF THE WEEK

The power of spiritual love is that it's instantly recognizable by those who experience it. There are times when you must take a stand even if it feels risky. Acting at such a high energetic level will work out in the best way for you.

TORI'S TIP

This week is about partnership and claiming your destiny. It's also about the power of spiritual collaboration. Regardless of the past or what will come, you must live your magnificent dream in the present.

MONDAY WEEK 49

THE FABLE OF BLACK AND WHITE

In Heaven, there meets a committee whose sole job is to decide the fate of those returning to Earth. These souls are waiting to go back (yet again) to complete their individual work. When it's time to return to Earth, they must leave and let go of relationships formed in Heaven. But while they're waiting to be reincarnated, the souls mingle and have fun.

One day, Black met White and it was magic. Soon they were rarely seen apart. They became concerned, however, when an elder warned them that they'd been ill-fated lovers in their last two lives. The Committee of Rebirth had already decided to keep them apart during their next incarnation, but Black and White wanted a chance for their love to work out. After hearing their request, the committee fell silent. No souls had ever before requested a change in their fate.

Judge Chang addressed them both, "Do you realize that you were meant to have an easier life this time and that together you may suffer?"

"And if you are together," added Judge Elijah, "White may not become a great poet as was chosen for this lifetime."

White looked at Black. They hadn't considered this.

Judge Chang waved his hand to dismiss their ridiculous notion. "Your choices have been made already."

Before his gavel hit the desk, White spoke. "If my life is choice, then I will be a great poet, but it is our fate that we ask you to reconsider."

White addressed the panel. "We ask that you grant us one more chance at our love as mortals."

"What of *your* fate?" Judge Chang asked Black.

"I'm not silent on that score because I'm being subservient," Black assured them. "I'm silent because my fate will unfold as it is meant to with White by my side."

"It shall be granted," said a voice larger than the chamber. The committee were silent in the presence of the Great Servant.

And so this outspoken pair were the first to force the members of the Committee of Rebirth to change their minds. On Earth White met Black and White indeed became the great poet that was fated long before.

And the day came when they toasted Black, too. Many nations would toast Black. White joked about being "First Spouse" when Black was sworn in as the first President of the United Earth.

First impressions: This fable is unequivocally about love and the risk we must be willing to take to be with someone we love. Even if there's no one in your life currently, they'll show up if that's what you seek. Expressing the force of nature that we call true love can make miracles happen.

Set your intention for the week: Consider this statement: "Together we are stronger than alone." This week, set your intention to *be* a stand. People talk about taking a stand, but being a stand is being like a rock, being truly in the intention you choose to create. There's no one to fight, nothing to defend. When you decide to be a stand, you're a powerful example of what's possible when you claim your destiny.

TUESDAY
COLOUR REFLECTION

What do Black and White say to you? Black is the shade that commands to be taken seriously. As it absorbs all the colours, it emits the warm, powerful energy of the protector. Unlike Black, White is alone and isolated. As it stands aloof, it does well to blend with the powerful Black. The purity of White resting alongside Black is a steadfast statement of truth. Light can't exist without dark. Consider the relationship of your yin to your yang. What must be balanced in you? When we're out of balance, we become sidetracked from our journey. Putting black and white together makes a powerful statement of our personal strength and balance.

Interestingly, in the illustration of this fable on page 206, blue and purple appear. In light of this, take some time today to reflect on how you communicate your deepest desires to the universe.

WEDNESDAY
JOURNAL JOURNEY

Find your inspiration: You have the ability to change the outcome, even if you can't predict exactly what that outcome may be. State your opinion. Step forward. The time is now.

This fable is also about the start of a brave new undertaking in which two powerful forces unite for the higher good. Perhaps a new path lies ahead of you.

Have you ever felt something in your heart so strongly that you know you must do it – but your brain tries to talk you out of it? If this fable resonates with you, you need to change old ways of thinking and take a stand. If you don't stand for something then you stand for nothing.

If this fable has stirred you, ask yourself: "Am I bold enough to take a risk?" When you've answered that question in your journal, write down the next question and answer it: "Do I dare to have my life the way I decide?" And finally, ask yourself: "Am I willing to sacrifice whatever it takes to have what I desire?" When you've finished, review what you wrote. Have you discovered anything new?

THURSDAY
MAKE A CONNECTION

Connecting with yourself and others: Today, take time to consider what you came here to do. What are you most sure of in your life? What do you know intuitively about destiny? Today's exercise will help you explore your ideas about destiny and then you'll be ready for Friday's meditation, in which you stand before the Great Spirits.

Solo exercise: What is your destiny? Is there something that you know is meant for you in this life? Take a few moments and write down whatever you have an inner knowing about. If this is challenging, begin with something obvious. For example, write: "I know that the sun will rise." Begin this way and continue until you feel satisfied with your list of what you know will happen for you in this life. Ask for support from the universe (you can do this in meditation or by asking a friend).

Group exercise: Everyone in the group writes down on a slip of paper the thing they most desire. Now put the papers in a bowl. Each person picks one - be careful not to pick your own. As you read the dream in front of you, describe the wonderful attributes of anyone who has a magnificent dream such as this. Who is this person really? What would the destiny be of someone who has a dream such as this? Offer empowering new ideas and beliefs to attach to the creation of this desire.

FRIDAY

MEDITATION MEANING

Going within: Can you find the meaning of your path? Once you've done the meditation, consider something you'd risk your life for. What is it? Step into the you that you must become to take a powerful stand and live an inspired life.

MEDITATION

Recall a time when you fought for something you believed in, and won. Allow the feeling of triumph to filter through your body. See yourself before the Council of the Great Spirits. Make a request. They will grant it if it's for the highest good of all. They tell you their decision. Thank the Spirits for their wise counsel. Relax in knowing that the council will confer with the Great Servant for you. You are welcome to go before the council anytime.

CONFUSION

Silver Cloud

This Week's Focus: Every silver lining has a cloud.

MESSAGE OF THE WEEK

Confusion forces us to stop and gives us the opportunity to think again about where we're going or to wait until a solution presents itself. How do you handle confusion in your life? Be aware that physical ailments, such as colds, express inner confusion and in some way are a form of resistance.

TORI'S TIP

If survival in the past included needing to know the answers, confusion can be a great struggle and feel very unsafe. This week consider how confusion can be an ally. In the fable, it's clear that Spirit is in the cloud, guiding and protecting Janna. When you feel confused, remember that you're actually being guided.

MONDAY WEEK 50

THE FABLE OF SILVER CLOUD

Janna climbed Faith Mountain for what felt like an eternity. Silver Cloud had descended upon her a few hours earlier and there was no way to tell how far she'd come or how much higher she had to go. When she began the journey, the sun had been shining but now dense fog surrounded her. It was cold and scary.

She thought about the previous day, when she'd left her boyfriend. There was another man waiting in the wings – there always was. Her own pattern of behaviour worried her. She'd felt called to climb Faith Mountain to try to understand her constant confusion.

The mist swirled around Janna. She felt frustrated. She wanted to sort out her feelings. Her head was full of questions. Should I have stayed where I was? Would he leave me? How can I know I've done the right thing?

Before Janna realized it, Silver Cloud had sneaked all around her and she was completely blinded. "Hey, I can't see!" she screamed.

"It was you who chose me," he told her, "for you choose not to see."

"What? Hey, who are you? *What* are you?" Janna spun around.

"I am Silver Cloud. I exist for those who do not wish to know the answers."

It took her a moment to accept that she was speaking to a cloud!

"I *am* confused," she admitted with a sigh.

"That is why you summoned me. I am your confusion. I will surround you until you choose to step into the light of awareness. Many enter my cloud to allow answers to come."

"But I want to know *now*," Janna cried.

He coughed out a billow of fog. "Answers will come when you are ready."

"When will I be ready?" Janna asked.

"When you are," came the reply.

"I knew that," she mumbled breathlessly and continued the climb. When she reached the top of the mountain, she stood for a long time in Silver Cloud, seeing nothing. She sat down and thought some more. Finally, she came to a decision. She'd return to the man who loved her dearly.

Silver Cloud slowly drew back to reveal the distant town, where somewhere a young man was heartbroken by his girlfriend's selfishness. Janna had journeyed farther than she'd realized.

She gasped. "Oh, Silver Cloud, thank you. If I'd had any idea how far I'd have to climb, I'd never have set out." But Silver Cloud had already dissolved and gone to assist someone else.

With her new self-understanding, Janna left the top of Faith Mountain. She began the long journey home to reclaim the love she knew awaited her.

First impressions: In this fable we begin to see how confusion is a tool. How many times have you used the phrase "I don't know", when somewhere deep inside you did know? Silver Cloud represents the truth that you've locked into a place of confusion. It's only when you feel safe that you can really ask yourself, "Do I really want to know the answer?" Be honest.

Set your intention for the week: This week, set an intention to observe how you've used confusion as a safe place to hide. When you find yourself feeling confused, ask yourself, "Is there something that I prefer not to look at?" Giving yourself permission to be confused will allow you the safety to open up when the time is right.

TUESDAY

COLOUR REFLECTION

What does Silver say to you? Silver is a sparkling neutral colour that resonates at a higher vibration than Grey. As a metallic, it has a powerful energy. Dazzling Silver speaks of integrity and fairness. It makes others respect you and seek your advice. It allows you to hold yourself with dignity, even when you don't know all the answers. Silver reflects a clean, truthful and solid way of being. Today, allow yourself to be in the unknowing space of Silver. Contemplate the elegance and power of Silver as you sit with Spirit and the unknown.

WEDNESDAY

JOURNAL JOURNEY

Find your inspiration: If confusion is a familiar state for you, then you already know Silver Cloud. Clarity is only available by journeying for a while in confusion.

If you knew how much work lay ahead, you might not undertake it. By masking your situation and asking simply that you carry on, Silver Cloud offers you marvellous opportunities. Clarity comes in its own good time. Silver Cloud is a reminder that we're guided in our confusion. There's nothing to solve here. Simply slow down and bide your time in gratitude and contemplation.

In your journal today, let's begin to reframe your experience of confusion. Write down how your life would change if confusion was simply a momentary pause with Spirit. Would you approach confusion as a blessing if you knew that on the other side you'd feel completely renewed? Take some time to think about these ideas and get to know the part of you that has made meaning around your confusion.

THURSDAY

MAKE A CONNECTION

Connecting with yourself and others: Today, in addition to doing an exercise, be conscious of saying "I don't know." When you find yourself repeating this phrase over and over, the real answer is that you *do* know but you're avoiding the perceived pain that knowing can bring. Rephrase to say, "I don't want to know", to give yourself more power and allow the truth to be revealed when you are ready.

Solo exercise: Ask yourself what confusion means to you. List the times in your life when perhaps you labelled panic as confusion. Have you noticed that when you've been in true confusion and allowed yourself space, the answer comes? In your alone time today, note down the occasions when you've triumphed through your confusion. Make a list of the things that you like to do when you're confused. That's right, sometimes you can tidy a sock drawer or do the dishes or watch your favourite movie and allow confusion like a cloud to pass by! Work with this concept today: Being solo doesn't mean being unsupported.

Group exercise: When confusion strikes, we can become desperate trying to work out our dilemma intellectually. Instead, thank your confusion. It has come as a friend to help your mind reset. Embrace your confusion, knowing that an answer will come in its own time. With this in mind, make a pro/con list about something you're confused about. Share this list with the group. Now create a pro/con list about the ideal circumstances regarding the same situation. Share again. Which one do you prefer to live with? Choose the list you want. Remember: Your job is the "what" not the "how." Allow the "how" - the way this is going to manifest - to take care of itself. Did anyone in the group have an "Ah ha!" moment, an insight that can help you see something clearly?

FRIDAY

MEDITATION MOMENT

Going within: By inviting confusion into your space, you allow stillness to expand. And in stillness authentic manifestation takes place. The more you expand stillness with Spirit, the more you'll find the answers come to you.

MEDITATION

Close your eyes and visualize the room you are in. Focus on one object in the room. When you are relaxed, sense the presence of Silver Cloud. Stay focused on the object as Silver Cloud completely engulfs you. When the object is no longer visible in your mind's eye, relax even more deeply and breathe. You are in the place of not knowing. It is a completely safe environment. Ask for the highest good and this shall be revealed - maybe not now, but soon.

CREATION

She Shaman

This Week's Focus: I will guide you to your muse.

MESSAGE OF THE WEEK

In the final fable we're given the gift of our own intuitive creation. She Shaman offers you a path into the artist's journey and reminds you that you already have everything you need. Every tool that you've gained, every fable that you've absorbed, every angel that has journeyed with you this year will always be with you.

TORI'S TIP

In this final, highly intuitive week of our journey together, She Shaman comes forward to show you how to use the spiritual toolkit that you've gathered. We return full circle to the conversation that took place in the red chakra about bringing your creativity into the Earth plane. This is your legacy. Your voice is now heard.

MONDAY

WEEK 51

THE FABLE OF SHE SHAMAN

When the world was a young child, it was very impressionable. There were plenty of ideas that hadn't yet been "done already." It was a time of trial, error and risks. It was a time when a person would create out of necessity – others were also creating out of necessity, so everyone was too busy to dismiss anyone else's idea as stupid or foolish.

It was a time when the trees and plants were free and not bought and sold. Time was told by the sun and teaching was something that the Great Spirits did. There was much work to do. There were not yet any great brains to think up hatred, revenge or war.

This was the time when She Shaman walked the Earth. She was revered as a Great Spirit. It was from her that you received the artist's calling. If she came to your village and chose you, well ... you were destined to be a great artist. One day, on a mountainous track between villages, She Shaman sat down and leaned against a cantankerous old tree to rest. Old Birch coughed loudly, startling She Shaman, who leapt up.

"Heh, heh, heh," giggled Birch. "I scared you, great She Shaman."

She Shaman laughed. "Yes, gifted elder, you did." And with that, she started away. "Hey," said Birch, "Wait!"

She Shaman stopped.

"I want my muse, too! It's never too late you know. I mean, my bark isn't what it used to be, but I can tell great tales. I also sing."

She Shaman was entertained for a long time by Birch's singing and story-telling. She smiled upon him and touched his flaking bark. "Oh, my great friend. You've had your art all along."

On that mountain it was decided. She Shaman vowed that she'd no longer choose which people were to receive a muse. She'd give *everyone* his or her own gift. She might, after all, overlook the gifts of another being as talented as old Birch.

And so to this day, we each have our own talents, no longer needing to wait for She Shaman to bring them to us. Oh, She Shaman still exists – she's there in every work of art and every creative connection, but she no longer walks the Earth plane.

Or does she?

First impressions: When we were children, we looked to others for our survival. This fable explores the idea of waiting for someone else to give us permission or approval to do something. It also shows how we can push back energetically – She Shaman is given feedback and she listens and changes for ever. Your personal creative expression is yours alone to do with as you wish.

Set your intention for the week: She Shaman reminds you that you have everything you need to create whatever you desire. This week, set an intention to think about how you can use all the tools you've gathered during this past year to forge ahead on your own path. Remember, She Shaman has already given you your gift. Which of your four grandparents has given you a legacy?

TUESDAY
COLOUR REFLECTION

What does She Shaman say to you? She Shaman is the colour of wine, reminding us that what's from the earth must remain connected to the earth. You need to communicate from a place of authenticity, because this colour represents the actualization of your soul and your ability to grow into your legacy. Today, acknowledge the gifts from your ancestors and remember that we didn't inherit anything from the past; rather, we're borrowing from the future. What will it take for you to live your reality in this present moment?

WEDNESDAY
JOURNAL JOURNEY

Find your inspiration: She Shaman whispers to you "Don't be like old Birch and wait for someone else to tell you of your muse. Connect with it!" This is your destiny calling. Anyone can choose an artistic path. The universe is waiting for you to begin your dance and express your love in a tangible form. Your art may take the form of a painting or sculpture, a short story or a song, a carefully prepared meal or a well-drafted life plan. If the fable of She Shaman resonates with you, know that you've cleared a channel for the Great Spirits to work with you. Dance! Rejoice!

Don't seek anyone else's opinion to confirm what you already know to be true inside. Don't wait for permission to act. You must trust your instinct and act from the voice within. The time to act is now, the moment has arrived. Let go of any need for approval and instead go within to seek your own answers. You will not be alone; She Shaman is there with you.

You're at a turning point as an artistic and expressive being. Today, write in your journal about the creative soul inside you. What will it take for you to live your artistic expression? Have you learned this year that you're ready? Write down the answers to these questions and make sure you include your angels and guides in the discussion.

THURSDAY
MAKE A CONNECTION

Connecting with yourself and others: If you've ever had a moment when the world disappeared as you lost yourself in a task, then you've experienced the creative zone. In working with this immersive energy you'll find your artistic muse. Use this as a starting point, but if writing or decorating or gardening is your thing, start there.

Solo exercise: Recall a time when you were in a creative zone. Take a few minutes to write down what you were doing, how you were feeling and any other sensory recall you have about the situation. Now, make notes about a creative project you wish to begin. How can you apply your positive experience of the past to the present? Meditate with She Shaman and afterwards start with a small creative step to propel you into a positive mindset. For example, if you have an idea for a painting, start by experimenting with combinations of paint colours. Don't worry about what you're painting initially, just get paint onto paper and see what happens!

Group exercise: Are you waiting for permission? Before you is old Birch. On the magical branches of this tree are answers to the following questions:

- What is my gift?
- Am I ready to face my gift?
- What would it take for me to create a breakthrough?

In this exercise, you have the chance to choose an answer to one of these questions. Each group member writes out answers to each of the three questions on separate pieces of paper. Write the question on the outside of the folded paper, so that it's visible. Gather the papers in three piles, according to the question, on a table. Each person then picks one piece of paper, making sure it's not one they wrote themselves. Now go around the room and welcome in the magic of Spirit as you read the answers. What do you learn?

FRIDAY

MEDITATION MOMENT

Going within: Our meditation calls forward the spirit guide She Shaman. Take some time to seek her wisdom about your gifts. Make sure you write down what she says, for she's here to support you but only for a short time; she has been summoned elsewhere.

MEDITATION

Open a notebook to a clean page. Close your eyes and imagine She Shaman standing in the mist, holding out her hand. Follow her – where you go is up to you. As you walk she motions for you to sit. Do so and ask for her guidance. Pick up your notebook and write. Simply write whatever comes. Do not censor or judge the words. They may not mean anything right now, but they will. Thank She Shaman for her visit.

CONCLUSION

You Did It!

MESSAGE OF THE WEEK

Congratulations – you've made it to the final week! If you're reading this, you've experienced standing still and allowing yourself to be loved. Each of the 49 fables has reflected your own darkness, dawn and light. You've probably noticed how some of the seemingly challenging fables became your pathway into the light, and how your perception of them changed, so that instead of seeing them as something that inspires dread, you came to know them as uplifting. As you take this work out into the world, remember that you now have a set of powerful tools to support you in facing whatever occurs in your life.

TORI'S TIP

This week, allow yourself to experience the bittersweetness of endings. As you reflect on the past year, remember how the best way to approach each fable or tool was not with the mind to understand it, but with an open heart to experience it. Remember this approach; you will find that an open heart is one of the most wonderful gifts you can bring to any relationship.

MONDAY — WEEK 52

THE POWER OF THE LIGHT

One of the most powerful things you can do is step into your own light. I've spoken before about darkness, dawn and light. In this final week I want you to understand that every phase is necessary. We can't skip our own darkness.

Have you ever asked someone how they're feeling and through clenched teeth they respond, "I'm OK"? Not very convincing, is it? But that's how many of us have tried to go through life. The world is full of people creating what I call a spiritual bypass. That's the state in which you jump to a false acceptance of circumstances. It's true that we can learn to move through these three phases at a different pace than we did in the past, but make no mistake: each one is vital.

The concept of stepping into the light is not about suddenly becoming elevated in everything that we do and always living in the light. That's not authentic – that's not the world we live in. For me, stepping into the light means knowing that I can be in my darkness for just as long as I need to be. I can accept that; I know that there are times when the darkness is the only place from which I can access my creativity. I allow myself to stay where I need to stay until I'm ready for the next step. And knowing that is the gift that I love to give others. When you do finally step into the dawn, there's an internal "hooray!" There's a sense that you did it, you crossed that finish line, you are committed to your own awakening.

Stepping into the light means being truly empathic. It doesn't mean understanding that you have all the answers, but instead realizing that you really don't. Then your life becomes an opening of inquiry. We ask, we observe and then we know.

- Ask = *darkness* = inquiry
- Observe = *dawn* = inquiry
- Know = *light* = trust

Your knowing and your personal evolution to this knowing come from the magic of the fables – and from your personal commitment to living intuitively.

Consider the power of the light. I invite you to absorb fully the idea that none of the fables, reflections and ideas in this book are positive or negative in themselves and that they never say anything about you except what you make them mean. You've learned step by step that you can choose a different perspective and a new way of being, if it suits you. Every one of the tools you've gained here in the form of life lessons will help you adjust your perspective.

The concept of allowing ourselves to step into the light or the highest good of a fable is interesting. Are we willing to live our highest spiritual potential? If you allowed yourself this experience in this past year, then I believe you've developed your intuition way beyond its capacity when you started. You've learned not to *have* the answer but instead to *be* the answer.

You may want to pick up on some of the ideas about multi-generational healing that have featured in this book – perhaps a new journey starts here. The more I work with the fables and their associated colours and chakras, the more I've come to understand that these are all my pathway to learning and teaching multi-generational healing. Today, I use the fables to illustrate the hidden agreements that my clients have with their ancestors. This toolkit has given you everything you need to open yourself to clearing and healing hidden family agreements.

Set your intention for the week: Reflect back on the tools you've gathered and notice how you now have the mind not to understand them but to draw on them and use them as needed. This week, set an intention to observe and be aware of how and when you reach for the tools in your new toolkit.

TUESDAY
COLOUR REFLECTION

What does the colour of your choice say to you? Today, let one of the 49 chakra colours featured in this book come to you. Which one appears when you shut your eyes? Whatever colour you imagine, look back in the book to revisit its colour reflection. Open yourself to the message it may be giving you regarding your family predecessors and ancestors. In particular, do you feel you are learning anything about your grandparents?

WEDNESDAY
JOURNAL JOURNEY

Find your inspiration: The point of today is to master not closing the loop. Try not to draw any conclusion; open yourself to your true feelings, without expecting an answer. Look back over the year and be brave enough to pick the fable that you resisted most. You may even have skipped it – you know which one it is. Notice your own resistance and stay open to the experience.

A year ago, I was giving a seminar on chakra personality types, using the *Chakra Wisdom Oracle Cards*. I pulled a card for one particular person and told her that it was indicating that her lessons were in her third chakra of yellow. She immediately resisted and stated that she didn't even like yellow – it had to be wrong. However, when I showed her the card a strange look came over her face. A few moments later, she shared that this was the exact image of her spirit guide. Later she showed me how the image on the card was indeed almost identical to a picture someone had drawn years earlier of one of her spirit guides. She began to see that the tools of this particular fable were meant for her.

Keep in mind that resistance is the response of our instinct for survival. We always resist what we think may make us look bad or hurt us, when in reality our greatest gift is housed there.

Turn to the fable you resisted and look at the journalling task. Do it again now – or perhaps do it for the first time. When you've finished, ask yourself if you see why it challenged you in the past. What comes up?

THURSDAY
MAKE A CONNECTION

Connecting with yourself and others: Today, you work with the idea of declaring something complete. So often, we keep things open-ended so as not to face the idea of finishing something. Endings are often fraught with memories of loss. In the solo activity you look at how you approach completion; in the group activity you practise saying goodbye.

Solo exercise: Take some time today to write about our journey together. Note the highs and lows, and most importantly allow yourself to declare your journey complete, so you can make room for the next adventure. Explore on paper how declaring something over and moving on can be uplifting and empowering.

Group exercise: In this meeting, all group members take turns saying goodbye to each other. This is your chance to declare the experience complete while you acknowledge and appreciate each person's contribution. Go around the room and thank each person for what they brought to the community. Each group member thanks everyone, then declares the journey complete for them. Finally, each person shares what they really feel about declaring something complete. Be open to each person's unique point of view. When one group ends, it offers the possibility for a new one to begin. Starting over brings you back to the red chakra.

FRIDAY

MEDITATION MEANING

Going within: This meditation is on completion. There is no one way to declare something finished. It's only important that, when we do so, we allow Spirit to take what's completed away, leaving space for the miracle of the new.

MEDITATION

Take a few moments to be with yourself, in this quiet space, allowing white light to surround you. Think of this journey you've been on and declare it complete. You have finally arrived home; notice how you are inside your own soul. Your legacy is already within you. The person you are now is stronger and more open to being in a state of loving. Your mind's eye sees yourself walking into the light, taking your angels and guides with you.

INDEX OF FABLES

ACKNOWLEDGMENTS

I must thank the tireless commitment of my editor, Fiona Robertson, who went above and beyond to bring this book forward for all of us; and Jo Lal, an incredible publisher who had the vision to see the value of this work for others.

It is my sincere wish that you use this material for your personal upliftment and share your blessings with others.

ABOUT THE
CHAKRA WISDOM ORACLE CARDS

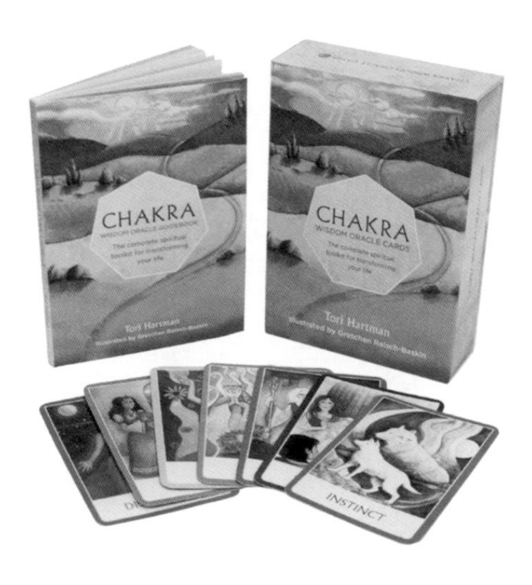

Your journey with the magic of the Chakra Wisdom Oracle continues ...

... when you use this toolkit along with the *Chakra Wisdom Oracle Cards*. As you add the cards to your intuitive toolkit, you'll see more synchronicity show up in your life, you'll get faster results in your work and you'll experience unimagined levels of connection with yourself, Spirit and others. These cards are a powerful way to set your intentions and live intuitively in order to achieve your dreams with ease.

Each of the 49 cards connects with a major chakra and represents one of the angelic fables in this book. The workbook includes divination spreads, chakra-by-chakra insight to guide you on your journey, and a personal inquiry and focused meditation for each card. The divination spreads range from basic one-card readings to more complex, yet still easy-to-use layouts.

To learn more about the cards and toolkit and to connect with others in the Chakra Wisdom Oracle community visit: **www.ChakraWisdomOracle.com**

"I ADORE these cards. They are immensely valuable for shifting perspective and creating profound new growth." SARK, Author, Artist, Succulent Wild Woman

ABOUT THE AUTHOR

Tori Hartman is a world-renowned intuitive and spiritual teacher. Her motto, "*Enlightenment Made Simple*", refers to her desire to give people the support they need in order to do spiritual work on their own. Born and raised in the free-thinking atmosphere of New York's Greenwich Village in the 1960s, Tori has been aware of her psychic abilities since the age of eight. A series of encounters with angels that began 25 years ago, after a near-death experience, revealed the profound fables that were to form the basis of the *Chakra Wisdom Oracle Cards*. These brightly-coloured fables became the backdrop for Tori's life-long fascination with colour and its power to transform and heal lives. Tori is based in Los Angeles, California.